LITURGICAL MINISTRY

A Practical Guide to Spirituality

Donna M. Cole

Resource Publications, Inc.
San Jose, California

Editorial director: Nick Wagner
Prepress manager: Elizabeth J. Asborno

Reprint Department
Resource Publications, Inc.
160 E. Virginia Street #290
San Jose, CA 95112-5876
(408) 286-8505 (voice)
(408) 287-8748 (fax)

Library of Congress Cataloging in Publication Data
Cole, Donna, 1962-
   Liturgical ministry : a practical guide to spirituality / Donna M. Cole.
      p.   cm.
   Includes bibliographical references (p.   ).
   ISBN 0-89390-372-8
      1. Lay ministry—Catholic Church. 2. Catholic Church—Liturgy. 3. Spiritual life—Catholic Church. I. Title.
   BX1916.C64   1996
   264'.02—dc20   96-8153

Printed in the United States of America

00 99 98 97 96 | 5 4 3 2 1

*For SGS, who taught me the meaning of trust and hope,
with thanks to all who taught, guided and formed me
along my own spiritual journey,
especially the staff and community
of St. Catherine of Siena, Cedar Grove, New Jersey,
both past and present.*

Contents

Foreword

A few years ago the Federation of Diocesan Liturgical Commission conducted a poll as to what was the most pressing challenge for the liturgical renewal. The response came as a surprise. The greatest challenge was perceived to be not what the liturgists expected, for example, the restructuring of rites or even the need for greater participation. It was rather the fact that people were out of touch with their religious experiences of God. Many worshipers appeared to be unable to relate what goes on at the Sunday eucharistic assembly with their lives during the rest of the week.

Liturgical Ministry: A Practical Guide to Spirituality addresses this need as it relates to the ministers of the Word, holy communion, music, hospitality, and serving. Donna Cole is eminently qualified for this task. She generously volunteers her time and talent as associate coordinator for liturgy at St. Catherine of Siena parish in Cedar Grove, New Jersey, where I serve as pastor. I know firsthand that she walks the talk. She finds her spirituality in the ministry she gives to the parish.

How does she do it? Donna tells us it begins with a call from God to serve the church. This call is what makes the difference between a liturgical functionary ("giving out communion") and a liturgical minister ("sharing the Eucharist"). This call leads to a spiritual identity as a minister, which includes a willingness to share more deeply with one's whole being in the paschal mystery of Christ we celebrate in the liturgy.

The liturgy is the public worship of the church. It was never intended to fulfill all our needs for prayerful communion with God. For this reason Donna offers suggestions from liturgical texts and from postures such as standing, sitting, kneeling, bowing, signing, and so forth in order to knit together personal prayer alone with personal prayer together (the sacred liturgy). In this way one is more in touch with an interior life so that a transition to common prayer is facilitated.

Foreword

In the chapter entitled "Call to Service" she addresses the particular challenge of being a lay minister in a world where you find yourself often unsupported by Christian values and must take the risk of appearing different by witnessing to Jesus Christ. This growth process toward discipleship calls for an ongoing discernment that flows from a vibrant spirituality. Her unpacking of the existential meaning of the renunciation and profession of faith at baptism is one of the highlights of the book.

What all this comes down to is the spirituality of the specific liturgical ministry: the various ministers find Christ in the very exercise of the ministry they perform in the service of their brothers and sisters in Christ. And what is more, they exercise their ministry properly to the extent that they animate the ministry of the assembly. Once the liturgical assembly is conscious of their sublime dignity that flows from baptism, they too are more eager to enter into the mystery of Christ dying and rising through their full, conscious, and active participation within the liturgy and by their commitment to go forth as a church with a mission to transform the world.

I am pleased to have been asked to write these few words which commend Donna's insights to a wider audience.

Very Rev. Charles W. Gusmer, STD,
Episcopal Vicar, Archdiocese of Newark

Preface

Like good stewards of the manifold grace of God, serve
one another with whatever gift each of you has
received. Whoever speaks must do so as one speaking
the very words of God; whoever serves must do so
with the strength that God supplies, so that God may
be glorified in all things through Jesus Christ. To him
belong the glory and the power forever and ever.
Amen (1 Pet 4:10-11).

In baptism each of us is called and challenged to join with
Christ, to become one with the community of believers, and
to share in the ministry of salvation. As our faith matures, we
are drawn to respond to that call by recognizing the gifts that God
has given us and discerning the ways in which they may best be
used in the service of God's people. For some, this is a conscious
choice, a decision with clear options—to follow or to turn away;
for others, it may mean a more subtle shift in life priorities. For
such a time of discernment to occur, we need an inner quiet, a
place where the whisper of the Holy Spirit can begin to be heard.
For many of us, this place is a tiny refuge of calm threatened
constantly by the turmoil and demands of our daily lives. This
book emerged out of a desire to support and nurture a life-long
journey of discernment by encouraging ways in which that "quiet
place of faith" can be allowed to grow and develop. This book is
devoted to those called to serve as liturgical ministers, for their
unique needs have often been neglected as their roles have
evolved. Empowered by the assembly to serve at liturgy, many
seek a higher level of spirituality or formational training and
discover that few materials are available which address their
specific concerns. Included here are scriptural texts, a few
thoughts as guides for reflection, and a focus on prayer that uses

the structure of our shared rituals to direct our spiritual preparation for service in ministry. Included also are adaptations of the texts of the commissioning rites of some of the ministries, as the words of these rites make important statements about ministry and are worthy of reflection. The final section considers the ways to apply this developing spirituality in a practical sense so that the service we offer may be transformed beyond mere function to an act of faith and love. Through these sections, this book has four primary objectives:

1. To focus actively and attentively on the call to ministry.

2. To nurture the connection between liturgy and everyday life.

3. To emphasize the spiritual foundation of ministry.

4. To present practical information on how (and how not) to serve at liturgy.

If the ministry of the liturgy is to grow and flourish, and it must if we as church are to survive, then it must be treated with the care and dignity deserving of any form of service to our God. I pray this collection is a step toward that end.

Acknowledgments

Scripture quotations are from the *New Revised Standard Version of the Bible*, copyright 1989 by the Division of Christian Education of the National Council of the Churches of Christ in the USA. Used by permission. All rights reserved.

Excerpts from the English translation of *Lectionary for Mass* © 1969, 1981, International Committee on English in the Liturgy, Inc. (ICEL); excerpts from the English translation of *The Roman Missal* © 1973, ICEL; excerpts from the English translation of *The Liturgy of the Hours* © 1974, ICEL; excerpts from the English translation of *Rite of Commissioning Special Ministers of Holy Communion* © 1978, ICEL; excerpts from the English translation of *Documents on the Liturgy, 1963-1979: Conciliar, Papal, and Curial Texts* © 1982, ICEL; excerpts from the English translation of *Rite of Christian Initiation of Adults* © 1985, ICEL; excerpts from the English translation of *Book of Blessings* © 1988, ICEL; excerpts from the English translation of *Ceremonial of Bishops* © 1989, ICEL; used with permission. All rights reserved.

Excerpts taken from *This Holy and Living Sacrifice* Copyright © 1985 United States Catholic Conference (USCC), Washington, DC 20017, are used with permission. *Music in Catholic Worship* Copyright © 1983 (USCC) and *Liturgical Music Today* Copyright © 1982 (USCC). A complete copy of each publication may be ordered by calling USCC Publishing Services (800) 235-8722.

Some of the considerations in the "Active Ministry" section were developed in conjunction with Rev. Bruce Janiga, a priest of the Archdiocese of Newark in the process of training and forming liturgical ministers.

Some of the thoughts in the "Servers" chapter (under Practical Considerations) stem from a personal communication with Rev. Thomas Iwanowski, Director of the Worship Office of the Archdiocese of Newark, New Jersey.

Call
and
Response

The call to ministry comes suddenly and unexpectedly to some. For others it is the next step in the natural progression of their faith journey. Some are called specifically to liturgical ministry. They find that liturgical ministry fills a need in their hearts to profess their faith in a public way as they extend a service to the community. Still others find themselves involved in service without a clear understanding of how they were drawn into it. Regardless of how it comes to be, many of those who are called to minister at liturgy had never considered serving in this way. Some feel unworthy; others are afraid or confused about what exactly they are being asked to do; many wonder what "authority" they have to do these things. Without a foundation of faith formed in prayer, it is impossible to function as a liturgical minister: anyone may read the Word—not all can proclaim it; any musician can play liturgical music—not all can make it come alive in the Spirit; anyone can open doors or take up a collection—not all can welcome the timid or encourage the uncertain; anyone may assist at the altar—not all can serve in a way that lends dignity and grace to a celebration; any person might be able to "give out communion"—not all can bring the living Body of Christ to those who are the Body of Christ. In speaking of liturgical ministers, the *Constitution of the Sacred Liturgy* (CSL) emphasizes that "they ought to discharge their office, therefore, with the sincere devotion and decorum demanded by so exalted a ministry and rightly expected of them by God's people" (29). The church speaks of the importance of the liturgy: "the liturgy is the summit toward which the activity of the Church is directed; at the same time it is the font from which all the Church's power flows. ...The liturgy in its turn moves the faithful, filled with 'the paschal sacraments,' to be 'one in holiness'; it prays that "they may hold fast in their lives to what they have grasped by their faith..." (CSL 10). The CSL continues to emphasize in a later section the primacy of the ministry of the assembly:

> The Church, therefore, earnestly desires that Christ's faithful, when present at this mystery of faith, should not be there as strangers or silent spectators; on the contrary, through a good understanding of the rites and

prayers they should take part in the sacred service
conscious of what they are doing, with devotion and
full involvement. They should be instructed by God's
word and be nourished at the table of the Lord's body;
they should give thanks to God; by offering the
immaculate Victim, not only through the hands of the
priest, but also with him they should learn to offer
themselves as well; through Christ the Mediator, they
should be formed day by day into an ever more perfect
unity with God and with each other, so that finally God
may be all in all (CSL 48).

This is the ministry of the celebrating community, and we who are
drawn to service from this community are challenged to clothe
ourselves in this liturgy as we explore our own spiritual selves. In
probing the different dimensions of ministry, it becomes clear that
the call to service in ministry includes a call to a deepening
spirituality of prayer and discernment as well as a call to action.

Call to Spirituality

If any want to become my followers, let them deny
themselves and take up their cross daily and follow
me. For those who want to save their life will lose it,
and those who lose their life for my sake will save it
(Lk 9:23-24).

The call to spirituality requires in response that we give
up the lives which belong to this world and give
ourselves in service to our Lord. We are not asked to
offer what we can spare in our lives but rather to empty our hearts
of all which separates us from the poverty of the cross. Ministry is
neither a beginning nor an end but rather a timeless component of
our communal journey of faith. Before we commit to serving in a
liturgical sense, we must first commit to lives of questioning,
examining the motivations and desires of our hearts, for the life of
a minister of Christ is one of dynamic, living faith. As we begin to
function in service to the liturgy, which defines our identity as
Catholic Christians, it is essential for us to scrutinize the way we
live and worship. We are challenged to embrace a new
understanding of the ways in which the ritual life of the church
impacts on our individual lives. At the same time we open our
hearts to a new humility as we place ourselves at the service of
others at prayer. A conscious desire for this openness is the first
step to a deep spirituality for it evokes in us a certain sense of
vulnerability; from this vulnerability ultimately comes the ability to
trust in Christ and in one another. As disciples of our Lord, we are
bonded to the body of all life and creation; we share in the dyings
and risings of all. As we reach out in service to our sisters and
brothers, we must risk loving as Christ has loved us—
unconditionally. Increasing our sensitivity to the breath of the Holy
Spirit leads to a greater awareness of the presence of God within

each of us. As we cultivate an active and faithful prayer life, we continue to nourish our own sense of spirituality by listening to the voice of God.

Call to Prayer

So I say to you, Ask, and it will be given you; search, and you will find; knock, and the door will be opened for you. For everyone who asks receives, and everyone who searches finds, and for everyone who knocks, the door will be opened (Lk 11:9-10).

The call to prayer naturally follows the call to a deeper spirituality: the first opens the way to questioning; the second opens the way to truth. In seeking the Lord, we invite Christ to open our eyes, our hearts, and our minds to the wonders of the kingdom. To serve the people of God, we must first be open to the power of the Spirit working in us and among us and be unafraid to listen in the stillness of prayer. Prayer is essential in the life of every Christian, but as ministers of the liturgy we are called to an even deeper dimension of prayer. Time for daily prayer must be a priority. The *General Instruction of the Liturgy of the Hours* (GILOTH) speaks clearly of this:

> Jesus has commanded us to do as he did. On many occasions he said: "Pray," "ask," "seek," "in my name." He gave us a formula of prayer in what is known as the Lord's Prayer. He taught us that prayer is necessary, that it should be humble, vigilant, persevering, confident in the Father's goodness, single-minded and in conformity with God's nature. The apostles have handed on to us, scattered throughout their letters, many prayers, especially of praise and thanksgiving. They warn us that we must be urgent and persevering in prayer offered to God in the Holy Spirit through Christ. They tell us of its sure power in sanctifying and

speak of the prayer of praise, of thanksgiving, of
petition and of intercession on behalf of all (5).

While the Liturgy of the Hours is by no means the only way to
establish a prayer routine, prayer of this format has the undeniable
advantage of forming a connection with the church throughout the
world, as Christians pray without ceasing on the never-ending
journey that begins and ends with Christ. "Then Jesus told them a
parable about their need to pray always and not to lose heart" (Lk
18:1). The church has been faithful in obeying this instruction; it
never ceases to offer prayer (GILOTH 10). The Liturgy of the
Hours is one way in which to internalize the hours and seasons
as we begin to embody that sense of timelessness which defines
our Christian faith.

> The Liturgy of the Hours extends to the different hours
> of the day the praise and thanksgiving, the
> commemoration of the mysteries of salvation, the
> petitions and the foretaste of heavenly glory, that are
> present in the eucharistic mystery, "the center and
> apex of the whole life of the Christian community." The
> Liturgy of the Hours is an excellent preparation for the
> celebration of the Eucharist itself, for it inspires and
> deepens in a fitting way the dispositions necessary for
> the fruitful celebration of the Eucharist: faith, hope, love,
> devotion and the spirit of self-denial (GILOTH 12).

Such preparation seems fitting for a minister of the liturgy, but
whatever the means, establishing a prayer routine helps to focus
prayer time and lends a continuity to meditation. Reflection on the
Sunday readings throughout the week is a good practice for all
who serve and is a simple way to initiate a prayer pattern. A more
ritualized pattern might include praying the Liturgy of the Hours or
one of the many modified versions of the Hours, either alone or
with others. *Catholic Household Blessings & Prayers* contains a
multitude of prayers for various seasons and occasions and
represents another way to focus prayer as relative to specific life
events. Making a personal commitment to read and reflect on one
of the Gospels during a particular season is a good way to
motivate Scripture-based prayer.

Another way to expand a prayer experience is to explore the
richness of the texts of our common prayers. These words,
prayed deliberately and with reflection, can serve as a useful

structure for individual meditation. Texts such as the Gloria, the Creed, and the Lord's Prayer become so routine that it is easy to lose the meaning of the words; praying these more deliberately, with attention to particular words or phrases, can open up new levels of meaning. For example, meditation each day on a single line of the prayers mentioned above may lead to a more personal understanding of words we often speak without hearing. The texts of many of the songs we pray at liturgy speak powerfully of the underlying Scripture; psalm responses can be an excellent focus for prayer. *Catholic Household Blessings & Prayers* contains prayers for many situations and occasions and is a wonderful source of daily prayers.

A creative way to connect personal prayer with ministry is to consider the various postures, gestures, and interactions of our common liturgy and to use these as a framework for prayer. Standing, sitting, and kneeling each holds different connotations with respect to prayer. Praying the same text on different days in different postures may lead to a new appreciation of the role of these postures in liturgy. Some of the other elements of our shared prayer life, such as bowing, signing, genuflecting, processing, greeting, embracing, receiving, and sharing, evoke different significance, emotions, or associations which can also be integrated into a prayer experience. Different environments (outdoor versus indoor prayer, for example) can change the "feel" of a prayer. Some of these options are explored in more detail in later sections, but the actual form of prayer is not of great significance. Various forms will be more appropriate than others at different points on the faith journey. What is most important is making the time for the silence and solitude that allow our hearts and minds to prepare to experience the paschal mystery in our own lives. Only by this experience of inner silence can our prayer progress and mature into active service. Our senses are overwhelmed with the noise of a world in chaos; in choosing silence, we turn away from the demands of this life and embrace the life of the world to come.

Call to Service

Follow me (Jn 1:43).

To serve one another as Christ has shown us by example is the greatest gift we can offer. As we struggle to follow Jesus, we grow closer to the glory of heaven, but at the same time we draw nearer to the sacrifice of the cross. As we minister to the people of God, we learn to rejoice in the sacrifices we are called to make as we pass through that cross in order to become one with the entire Body of Christ. Lay ministry involves a struggle, and this struggle sets us apart.

We are called to be living examples of faith, to embrace discipleship as a way of life, while living and working in a world where our values are often considered to be valueless. It is a challenge to avoid living two separate lives. Being a Christian is not difficult when we are among only those who believe. It becomes an entirely different task when we walk into the workplace on Monday morning and attempt to be the same people we were on Sunday morning. It is much easier to live two different lives—one for church and one for the rest of the time. In doing this we deny our own Christian identity. We begin to arbitrarily divide the world into two conflicting territories—the sacred and the profane. Creation has no such boundaries. As a people of God, we are called to recognize, welcome, and embrace the presence of the divine all around us, in every time and place. We then realize that the sacred surrounds us while the "profane" fades into obscurity in the presence of the God who in Christ shattered the power of darkness.

Every day we are challenged to live what we believe. While this general concept applies to a wide variety of situations, as liturgical ministers we are called especially to live the seasons of the church. It is senseless to celebrate the hopeful tensions of the

Advent season at liturgy if our homes and offices speak only of
Christmas. And how can we prepare our hearts and minds for the
joy of the Easter season if our Lenten disciplines take place only
at home or when we are alone in our rooms at prayer? What of
the witness value that is lost when we scrub the ashes from our
faces, or postpone our fasting until after the office party, or work
without question or interruption on Good Friday because to do
otherwise would label us as "different" and draw unwanted
attention to ourselves? Bearing witness to the faith that we as
Catholic Christians profess is an integral part of ministry. Just as
we set the example for the assembly at liturgy, we are called to be
an example of Christ at home and in the world. Called to be the
presence of Christ in the same world which rejected his message
of justice presents us with a challenge of enormous potential. We
who are chosen in baptism are asked each day to choose the
path we will follow.

The following text is from a homily on the Acts of the Apostles
by Saint John Chrysostom, bishop, adapted from the *Office of
Readings* from the "Common of Holy Men." The responsory which
follows is an appropriate focus as we begin to examine the call to
service.

> There is nothing colder than a Christian who does not
> seek to save others.

> You cannot plead poverty here; the widow putting in
> her two small coins will be your accuser. Peter said:
> *Silver and gold I have not.* Paul was so poor that he
> was often hungry and went without necessary food.

> You cannot plead humble birth, for they were humbly
> born, of humble stock. You cannot offer the excuse of
> lack of education, for they were uneducated. You
> cannot plead ill-health, for Timothy also had poor
> health, with frequent illnesses.

> Each one can help his neighbor if only he is willing to
> do what is in his power. Look at the trees that do not
> bear fruit: have you not noticed how strong and fine
> they are, upstanding, smooth and tall? If we had a
> garden, we would much prefer trees with fruit—
> pomegranates and olives—to trees that are for

pleasure, not for utility, and any utility these have is small.

Do not say: it is impossible for me to influence others. If you are a Christian, it is impossible for this not to happen. Things found in nature cannot be denied; so here, for it is a question of the nature of the Christian.

The light of a Christian cannot escape notice. So bright a lamp cannot be hidden.

RESPONSORY

Be pure and intent of heart, bent on him, the holy One, who has called you;
—be holy in all you do.

I am your own God, your Lord;
be holy for I am holy.
—Be holy in all you do.

Discernment

Be holy in all you do (Responsory, "Common of Holy Men," *Office of Readings*).

Through prayer we come to recognize the whisper of the Holy Spirit within us. Having determined to listen, a choice remains. Now we must choose the direction of that first uncertain step on the path of service.

This is discernment; this is the ongoing struggle of wondering, the inward-looking time of asking who it is we are called to be. As surely as we are born, and as certainly as we must some day die to live again, each of us has a role to play in the great plan of salvation. That role is ever-evolving, and that evolution demands that we attend with our heart and all our senses to textures and aromas, to light and darkness, to silence and noise, to order and chaos, to sadness and joy, to death and resurrection. Only in this way may we find our place in a creation which is at once elegantly simple and rich in complexity. In liturgy we assemble these elements of creation and find a place for each. The same is true in our own lives, for it is only as our awareness of the wonder of creation grows that we may begin to find our own place among them. As we begin to discover this identity, the call to ministry may become clear for an instant. Grasping that instant is the challenge. Whatever else we do, this much is certain: if we seek holiness at all times and strive to live always in the example of Jesus Christ, we cannot fail to glorify God. The following text, a suggested reading for the rites of initiation, emphasizes and defines our Christian identity:

> Blessed be the God and Father of our Lord Jesus Christ, who has blessed us in Christ with every spiritual blessing in the heavenly places, just as he chose us in

Christ before the foundation of the world to be holy and blameless before him in love. He destined us for adoption as his children through Jesus Christ, according to the good pleasure of his will, to the praise of his glorious grace that he freely bestowed on us in the Beloved. In him we have redemption through his blood, the forgiveness of our trespasses, according to the riches of his grace that he lavished on us. With all wisdom and insight he has made known to us the mystery of his will, according to his good pleasure that he set forth in Christ, as a plan for the fullness of time, to gather up all things in him, things in heaven and things on earth. In Christ we have also obtained an inheritance, having been destined according to the purpose of him who accomplishes all things according to his counsel and will, so that we, who were the first to set our hope on Christ, might live for the praise of his glory. In him you also, when you had heard the word of truth, the gospel of your salvation, and had believed in him, were marked with the seal of the promised Holy Spirit; this is the pledge of our inheritance toward redemption as God's own people, to the praise of his glory (Eph 1:3-14).

I implore you in the Lord,
lead a life worthy of the vocation to which you have
   been called.
—Be careful to preserve the unity of the Spirit
   in the bond of peace.

There is one body and one Spirit,
and there is but one hope given to you by your calling.
—Be careful to preserve the unity of the Spirit
   in the bond of peace
(Responsory, "2nd Sunday in Ordinary Time," *Office of Readings*; cf. Eph 4:1,3-4).

The
Prayer
of
Ritual

I therefore, the prisoner in the Lord, beg you to lead a life worthy of the calling to which you have been called (Eph 4:1).

I n choosing liturgical ministry as a way of life and form of
service, the time of discernment does not end. Discernment
continues as we are challenged to consider not only whether
to serve but also in what ways our service can be of the greatest
value. As ministers of the community at prayer, the liturgy itself
becomes a part of our own spirituality and life, in which each
element takes on deeper significance. The *Lectionary for Mass:
Introduction* (LMIn) professes that "the more profound our
understanding of the liturgical celebration, the higher our
appreciation of the importance of God's word. Whatever we say
of the one, we can in turn say of the other, because each recalls
the mystery of Christ and each in its own way causes that
mystery to be ever present" (5). As ministers of that liturgy, our
understanding of both the celebration and the celebrating
community is crucial. A particular challenge is to avoid allowing
our symbols and celebrations to become ordinary. In no sense
can the paschal mystery be ordinary. Every liturgy we celebrate,
eucharistic or not, is integrally connected to that mystery which
makes us one. All that we do and all that we are has its source
and purpose in that one act of sacrifice and salvation.

Everything that we do at liturgy has meaning. Ritual dialogue
and posture are two elements of our celebrations which we often
take for granted, and they may serve as a continuing focus for
individual prayer and growth. The images of the liturgies of
initiation are an appropriate starting point for a "rediscovery" of our
rites and rituals. Our own ministry proceeds from our baptism, but
rarely do we recall the commitment that was made at baptism,
affirmed at confirmation, and renewed each Sunday in the
Eucharist. The first question asked of us or of our parents or
sponsors when we are presented for baptism is, *"What do you
ask of God's church?"*—a simple question of profound
significance. It is a question we should consider anew as we
begin a life of service in ministry. As we begin our liturgical
ministry, a reevaluation of our expectations is in order. Just what
is it that we ask of God's church? The traditional response of
"baptism" is not quite in order, but it may be that what we ask is
not so very different. Perhaps as we grow in the life of the church,
what we should ask is to be immersed in the fire of the Spirit, to

be engulfed in living water, and to be renewed in our unity with the community of believers in Jesus Christ. In this way our ministry may always be a viable extension of the promise we make in baptism. In baptism we renounce sin and profess faith, and by this dialogue the faith of the church is embraced. In each Easter season we renew our promises of baptism. If we do not actively attend to them, they may lose their impact on our lives. But if we consciously commit to these promises, our faith will be immeasurably strengthened by the depth and power of these words. (The following questions are from the "Renewal of Baptismal Promises [at the Easter Vigil]," RCIA 238-239.)

> *Do you reject sin so as to live in the freedom of God's children?*

So often we mechanically answer "I do" without considering the import of what we have said. Avoiding sin is not the same as actively rejecting sin. We not only choose to reject sin in our own lives, but we dedicate ourselves to the rejection of sin in the world. This is the basis of our social conscience. This cannot be separated from liturgy and it cannot be ignored in our personal lives. To remain silent is not a rejection of sin and, in fact, may prevent us from living in the freedom of God's children. We are called in baptism to be living examples of the freedom promised us when we commit willingly to lives worthy of that call.

> *Do you believe in God, the Father Almighty,*
> *creator of heaven and earth?*

Such a simple question, but what profound depth is contained in these words. For in recognizing God as creator of all that is, we acknowledge that we who are formed in God's image are intimately connected to the kingdom of God. In Christ and with Christ, we span the distance between heaven and earth. In the same way, our sacraments connect us both to the created world and to the heavenly kingdom. The water of baptism is the water that surrounds us before birth, the water we drink to sustain life, and the water that consumes us with the wonder of life in Christ. When we answer "I do!" to this primary question, let it be with faith and conviction rather than out of habit.

> *Do you believe in Jesus Christ, his only Son, our Lord,*
> *who was born of the Virgin Mary,*
> *was crucified, died, and was buried,*

rose from the dead,
and is now seated at the right hand of the Father?

If we mechanically mumble "I do" in response to this, we deprive ourselves of the joy of committing to the faith we claim to profess. The way we answer this question defines who we are. Here is the challenge to profess what the world dismisses as nonsense: that a child was born of a virgin who was in fact the Son of God, that he labored in service to those lost in sin, that he gave his life in love, that he died, rose to live again, and reigns now with God for all eternity. When we acclaim "I do" to this belief, we reject the beliefs of this world and embrace the faith of Christ. As ministers of the church, we have just affirmed that we believe what we celebrate each week, that the liturgy for us is more than history; it is instead a living truth.

Do you believe in the Holy Spirit,
the holy catholic Church, the communion of saints,
the forgiveness of sins, the resurrection of the body,
and the life everlasting?

When we give our assent, we commit ourselves—heart, mind, and soul—to the faith of the church. In a real sense, this is our commissioning to ministry. We serve by virtue of our own baptism, and all that we are as a Christian people flows from the font that gives us life in Christ.

This is our faith. This is the faith of the Church. We are
proud to profess it, in Christ Jesus our Lord. Amen ("Rite of Baptism for Children" 59, *Rites*).

Exploring Faith
through Liturgy

This is our faith ("Rite of Baptism for Children" 59, *Rites*).

Our liturgy takes this faith that we profess and gathers with it all of our emotions, hopes and dreams, fears and failings, and joys and sufferings and forms them together into the worship which speaks of all these things. "[T]he effect of the liturgy of the sacraments and sacramentals is that almost every event...is made holy by divine grace that flows from the paschal mystery of Christ's passion, death, and resurrection, the fount from which all sacraments and sacramentals draw their power. The liturgy means also that there is hardly any proper use of material things that cannot thus be directed toward human sanctification and the praise of God" (CSL 61).

Our worship takes form not only in the words we speak and the praises we sing but also in the way we pray with our entire bodies. Our communal prayer is never passive; we stand in praise, kneel in penitence, walk in procession, embrace in reconciliation, and go forth as a people of peace to serve the world. Long-time Catholics may no longer notice these ritual movements because they have become automatic, almost reflex, to us. These movements merit greater attention for ministers of the liturgy. They can help us to focus our own prayer as well as help us to explore more deeply the symbols which help us to imagine the God whose simplicity and complexity is beyond the ability of our words to describe.

Nothing we do at liturgy should be routine. From the time we enter into our place of worship to the moment we go forth as a community to serve in the spirit of that prayer, every action should be deliberate. "It is an old and honored practice for all who enter a church to dip their hand in a font of holy water and sign themselves with the sign of the cross as a reminder of their baptism" (*Ceremonial of Bishops* 10). What a shame that so few stop to consider what we do when we perform this sacramental act. By this simple blessing we reaffirm our connection to baptism and to the entire Body of Christ. In the signing of ourselves with the cross, we also commit to the cross of Christ, to living as he has called us to live, to willingly carry the cross in and on our own bodies. With the following passage and reflection, consider your own response to the significance of this blessing and signing.

✠ Reflection

This is the one who came by water and blood, Jesus Christ, not with the water only, but with the water and the blood. And the Spirit is the one that testifies, for the Spirit is the truth (1 Jn 5:6).

- As I sign myself with this holy water, am I committed to the cross that I now trace on my own body?

- Will I embrace this commitment proudly and without shame?

- Can I allow this action to be a transition for me, a moment to slow down and consider who I am and what I am called to be in this time and place?

Blessed are you, Lord, all-powerful God,
who in Christ, the living water of salvation,
blessed and transformed us.
Grant that, when we are sprinkled with this water
or make use of it,
we will be refreshed inwardly by the power of the
  Holy Spirit
and continue to walk in the new life we received
  at baptism.
We ask this through Christ our Lord
("Order for the Blessing of Holy Water Outside Mass,"
Book of Blessings [BB] 1396).

As a liturgical minister, you will often take part in ritual procession. This, too, should be undertaken with a clear understanding and conscious attention to the movement. Procession at liturgy is not merely a way of moving people from place to place but is rather an expression of purpose and unity. At a eucharistic liturgy, we gather as a people of faith. The procession is a symbolic representation of our communal journey to the altar of sacrifice and salvation. This procession is led by the cross, the sign of our salvation, and we who believe follow that cross into the very presence of our God. Again our action can focus our prayer as we call to mind the ways in which our own faith journey leads us onward.

✢ Reflection

I will lead the blind
    by a road they do not know,
by paths they have not known
    I will guide them.
I will turn the darkness before them into light,
    the rough places into level ground.
These are the things I will do,
    and I will not forsake them (Isa 42:16)

- Do I hesitate with each step?

- Is my heart open to the guidance of the Holy Spirit?

- Will I allow myself to listen with my entire being, or do I trust only the senses of this world?

✢ ✢ ✢

The following is part of the Rite of Acceptance in which catechumens are signed with the cross. As with many other ritual prayers it may serve as a reminder of the people we are called to be and of the response we are called to make:

Receive the sign of the cross on your ears,
that you may hear the voice of the Lord.

Receive the sign of the cross on your eyes,
that you may see the glory of God.

Receive the sign of the cross on your lips,
that you may respond to the word of God.

Receive the sign of the cross over your heart,
that Christ may dwell there by faith.

Receive the sign of the cross on your shoulders,
that you may bear the gentle yoke of Christ.

Receive the sign of the cross on your hands,
that Christ may be known in the work which you do.

Receive the sign of the cross on your feet,
that you may walk in the way of Christ.

Almighty God,
by the cross and resurrection of your Son
you have given life to your people.
Your servants have received the sign of the cross:
make them living proof of its saving power
and help them to persevere in the footsteps of Christ.
We ask this through Christ our Lord
(adapted from RCIA 56, 57).

In procession, the next ritual action is to reverence the altar with
a bow. Reaching the altar we again use our bodies to express our
prayer. When we bow before the altar, we bring ourselves low in
reverence of that holy table. If we allow ourselves to experience
that posture it can evoke powerful emotion. This is not an action
that we employ in our ordinary lives. It implies a level of respect
and humility that we may find awkward or uncomfortable. This
bow reminds us that our approach to the sacrifice that defines
justice demands that we put aside trivial matters and focus our
entire being on reconciling that which is unjust in our own lives.

✠ Reflection

As no darkness can be seen by anyone surrounded by
light, so no trivialities can capture the attention of
anyone who has his eyes on Christ. The one who
keeps his eyes upon the head and origin of the whole
universe has them on virtue in all its perfection; he has
them on truth, on justice, on immortality and on
everything else that is good, for Christ is goodness itself
(excerpted from a homily on Ecclesiastes by St.

Gregory of Nyssa, bishop, "Monday of the 7th Week in Ordinary Time," *Office of Readings*).

- Do I recognize the call to justice in my own life?

- Are there those whom I have resisted forgiving?

- Do I struggle against forgiving myself?

- As I bow in reverence before this table of love, am I willing to embody the attitude of a servant?

- Will I put aside all that is trivial in this life that I may focus of the goodness of Christ?

- Can I offer all that I am in unity with this living sacrifice?

Blessed are you, Lord our God,
who accepted the sacrifice of Christ,
offered on the altar of the cross
for the salvation of the world.

Now with a Father's love,
you call your people to celebrate his memory
by coming together at this table.

May this altar be the table
at which we break the bread which gives us life
and drink the cup which makes us one.

May it be the fountain of the unfailing waters
    of salvation.
Here may we draw close to Christ,
the living stone,
and, in him, grow into a holy temple.

Here may our lives of holiness
become a pleasing sacrifice to your glory. Amen
(adapted from the "Blessing of an Altar," chapter 6, no.
9, *Rites*, vol. 2).

✛ ✛ ✛

Having now formed ourselves into a celebrating community, we mark ourselves with the sign of our salvation, making the sign of the cross over our entire selves as we proclaim that what we now do is in the name of the Father and of the Son and of the Holy Spirit. By this sign we identify ourselves as followers of Christ, as people who proclaim in word and action that the paschal mystery is reality. By this sign we focus our lives on the God who saves us. By this sign we pray for guidance and protection, strength and wisdom, blessing and sanctity. By this sign we begin and end all things. By this sign we ask for a share in the humanity and divinity of Christ. This signing is more than mere gesture; it is an act of commissioning, of offering, of devotion, and of prayer.

✚ *Reflection*

Think of these things when you make the sign of the cross. It is the holiest of all signs. Make a large cross, taking time, thinking what you do. Let it take in your whole being—body, soul, mind, will, thoughts, feelings, your doing and not-doing—and by signing yourself with the cross strengthen and consecrate the whole in the strength of Christ, in the name of the triune God (Guardini 114).

- As I make this sign of the cross, am I able to surrender my heart, mind, and body?

- Do I have the courage to stand at the foot of the cross and proclaim Jesus Christ as Lord and Redeemer?

- Will I proudly profess my faith when I leave this assembly?

- Can I offer all that I do in the name of the Father and of the Son and of the Holy Spirit?

- Is my "Amen" a reflex or do I truly affirm all that this implies?

As we look upon the cross, let us call to mind that on it Christ brought to completion the sacrament of his love for the Church.

As we bow before the cross, let us remember that in his own blood Christ has removed all divisions and out of the many nations created the one people of God.

As we venerate the cross, let us reflect that we are
ourselves Christ's disciples and must therefore follow
him, willingly taking up our own cross each day.

Lord,
your Son reconciled us to you
by suffering on the cross
and then returned to you in glory.

May we who embrace this cross as a sign
    of redemption
find in it protection and strength,
shouldering our own crosses
in the spirit of the Gospel
until our journey ends. Amen
(adapted from "The Blessing of a New Cross for Public
Veneration," BB 1241, 1242).

✠ ✠ ✠

Throughout our liturgy, our posture continues to reflect the
attitude of our prayer. We kneel in penitence, in adoration, in
contemplation, in hope. This is the most familiar of prayer
postures, the posture of the beggar, of those who plead for mercy
and forgiveness.

For this reason I bow my knees before the Father, from
whom every family in heaven and on earth takes its
name. I pray that, according to the riches of his glory,
he may grant that you may be strengthened in your
inner being with power through his Spirit, and that
Christ may dwell in your hearts through faith, as you
are being rooted and grounded in love. I pray that you
may have the power to comprehend, with all the
saints, what is the breadth and length and height and
depth, and to know the love of Christ that surpasses
knowledge, so that you may be filled with all the
fullness of God.
    Now to him who by the power at work within us is
able to accomplish abundantly far more than all we ask
or imagine, to him be glory in the church and in Christ
Jesus to all generations, forever and ever. Amen (Eph
3:14-22).

We sit as the Word of God is proclaimed among us not as spectators but as companions of our Lord, watching and waiting, open to the Word which comes to life and is fulfilled in our gathering.

> Then Jesus went with them to a place called Gethsemane; and he said to his disciples, "Sit here while I go over there and pray." He took with him Peter and the two sons of Zebedee, and began to be grieved and agitated. Then he said to them, "I am deeply grieved, even to death; remain here, and stay awake with me." And going a little farther, he threw himself on the ground and prayed, "My Father, if it is possible, let this cup pass from me; yet, not what I want, but what you want." Then he came to the disciples and found them sleeping; and he said to Peter, "So, could you not stay awake with me one hour? Stay awake and pray that you may not come into the time of trial; the spirit indeed is willing, but the flesh is weak" (Mt 26:36-41).

Filled with joy, we stand as our Alleluia acclaims the Word of the Lord broken open and shared among us. We rise as we proclaim the risen Christ as Lord and Savior. As we stand our bodies reflect both our awe of this great mystery and our own dignity as a Christian people, washed clean and called to be holy by the Word we now hear. We stand in unity with one another, a family of believers whose strength comes from the faith we share. We stand with those whose faith is weak, with those whose vision seems certain, with those who question, and with those who see truth, and we stand confident, one with all the saints, risen in the timelessness of Christ.

> Truly I tell you, if you say to this mountain, "Be taken up and thrown into the sea," and if you do not doubt in your heart, but believe that what you say will come to pass, it will be done for you. So I tell you, whatever you ask for in prayer, believe that you have received it and it will be yours. Whenever you stand praying, forgive, if you have anything against anyone; so that your Father in heaven may also forgive you your trespasses (Mk 11:23-25).

We embrace those with whom we have broken open the Word and shared the story of salvation as we struggle to recognize in each other the living Body of Christ. Here we may stretch the limit of our comfort; a handshake is far removed from a kiss of peace, but it may be the first step in breaking out of the isolation of our own private prayer experience. Here we have the opportunity to be truly present to each other, to be what we receive, but sadly we too often limit ourselves to the safety of distance. Touch communicates far more than words, reaching through pain and speaking of a desire for peace and reconciliation. Our relationships are defined in the way we touch each other. The church recognizes the power of touch in the laying on of hands, an ancient form of prayer and healing. Our contact with one another brings us closer to touching Christ, allows us to experience the wonder of his presence in our midst. It draws us to enter into the communion which makes us one, the communion that allows us to live in the house of the Lord, that communion which makes the paschal mystery both mystery and reality.

When finally we are sent forth from our community, we are called to embody the peace of Christ and to share the Good News with all the world. The eucharistic liturgy ends with the words, "The Mass is ended, go in peace to love and serve the Lord," followed by the assembly's response of praise. The Mass is ended, but the service is just beginning, as our time of service has neither beginning nor end. Although we are formed in prayer and our worship is a sort of "spiritual recharging," if our prayer does not call us to action in the name of the Lord, our ministry will have no meaning. It is empty and without substance; it is function without reason. In order for ministry to be real, we are called to take the words and ritual of prayer and transform them into the works that define us as Christians.

> Go therefore and make disciples of all nations,
> baptizing them in the name of the Father, and of the
> Son, and of the Holy Spirit, and teaching them to obey
> everything that I have commanded you. And
> remember, I am with you always, to the end of the age
> (Mt 28:19-20).

Transforming Faith
into Action

You see that a person is justified by works and not by faith alone. For just as the body without the spirit is dead, so faith without works is also dead (Jas 2:24,26).

The Holy Spirit calls us to prayer, this prayer fulfills faith, and this faith demands of us action in the name of Christ. When we say "yes" to ministry, we say "yes" to Christ and to all whom he claims as his own. In this way, a unity is formed between the essence of ourselves and all the people of God. Our prayerful preparation for ministry is crucial and necessary, but as ministers of the liturgy, we are called not only to pray but to practice what we pray. On one level, each ministry demands of us the same response—to allow Christ to live in us and to recognize and serve the very life of Christ in our sisters and brothers. But unless we also cultivate the practical skills which allow these ministries to take effective form, we cannot respond to this call. In practice, each ministry requires a slightly different focus to make this transition from faith to action.

Do you not believe that I am in the Father and the Father is in me? The words that I say to you I do not speak on my own; but the Father who dwells in me does his works. Believe me that I am in the Father and the Father is in me; but if you do not, then believe me because of the works themselves. Very truly, I tell you, the one who believes in me will also do the works that I do, and in fact, will do greater works than these, because I am going to the Father. In a little while the world will no longer see me, but you will see me;

> because I live, you also will live. On that day you will
> know that I am in my Father, and you in me, and I in
> you (Jn 14:10-12,19-20).

Some practical principles are common to all involved in serving at liturgy. Although most of the suggestions that follow are made in the context of a Mass, similar considerations apply to any type of liturgy. This section is not intended to be a comprehensive review of the tasks of each liturgical minister but rather some general thoughts that may be of help to those just beginning liturgical ministry.

A prompt arrival of no less than fifteen minutes before a liturgy is scheduled to begin allows each minister time to pray and prepare. This helps to foster a sense of a calm and peaceful preparation as well as to minimize the distractions of rushing through last-minute adjustments and instructions. Remember that your service is important and that others are depending on you. If you find you cannot serve a liturgy for which you have been scheduled, you should consider it your responsibility to arrange for a substitute or to contact the person responsible for scheduling liturgical ministers. Everyone involved should understand the liturgy to be celebrated. All should be aware of any ritual changes that may require special attention or care. Joining in prayer with the other liturgical ministers before the start of the liturgy helps to put aside distraction and to focus hearts and minds on the service we offer. In this way we enter into the presence of the Lord and of each other. In a sense we are all ministers of hospitality and as we continue our prayer and preparations we must also take the time to welcome those who come to worship. This should be a heartfelt welcome as we greet our own family in Christ.

As the liturgy begins, the procession forms in the order of crossbearer, servers, ministers of communion, readers, presider. Depending on the nature of the celebration, different people may be included, but the general order remains the same. As you take your place in the procession, enter into the celebration by joining in the gathering song. Use whatever worship aid is necessary. Your action is the model for the assembly; if your attitude is distant or unprayerful, you set a striking negative example. You have the opportunity to encourage the assembly in participation by your own active participation in all facets of the liturgy. Your involvement in the liturgy from gathering to sending forth is a strong witness to the power of prayer to impact on our lives.

Active
Ministry

Readers

In the beginning was the Word, and the Word was with
God, and the Word was God. He was in the beginning
with God. All things came into being through him, and
without him not one thing came into being. What has
come into being in him was life, and the life was the
light of all people. The light shines in the darkness, and
the darkness did not overcome it. And the Word
became flesh and lived among us, and we have seen
his glory, the glory as of a father's only son, full of
grace and truth (Jn 1:1-5,14).

✠ Introduction

You are called to proclaim the Word of God. You are a
storyteller, called to speak the words of salvation. First you must
learn the story so that when you share it, the Word will take life
and dwell among those who hear it. It is not enough just to read
the words on the page; this ministry requires, above all things, a
strong belief in and devotion to the Truth proclaimed in Scripture.
Your mission to proclaim the Word does not begin and end with
the celebration of liturgy; it is the natural extension of a Christian
life. While part of your role is to bring the words on the page to life,
these same words should become a part of your own life so that
day by day you may become a living example of the Word in
action.

The following passage is taken from a version of the "Rite for
the Institution of Readers," and it demonstrates the value the
church places on this ministry. Although this rite was intended for
use in the formal institution of men into the ministry of lector prior
to ordination to the diaconate, it has been used in modified form
to commission both men and women as readers, and it speaks
powerfully of the importance of the ministry of the Word:

Through His Son, God has revealed the mystery of
salvation and brought it to fulfillment. Jesus Christ
made all things known to us, and then entrusted His
Church with the mission of preaching the Gospel to the
whole world.

As readers and bearers of God's Word, you will assist
in this mission; you will be given a responsibility in the
service of the faith which is rooted in the Word of God.
You will proclaim that Word in the liturgical assembly.
You will bring the message of salvation to those who
have not yet received it. Thus, with your help, men and
women will come to know God our Father and His Son
Jesus Christ, and so be able to reach eternal life.

In proclaiming God's word to others, accept it yourself
in obedience to the Holy Spirit. Meditate on it
constantly, so that each day you will have a deeper
love of the scriptures, and in all you say and do show
forth to the world our Savior, Jesus Christ.

✢ Preparation

Your role in the Liturgy of the Word is crucial, and it is essential
that you approach it with sincerity and firm commitment. Most of
your preparation will take place well before the start of the liturgy
at which you minister. For example, if you read at Sunday
Eucharist, it may be helpful to include the readings which you will
proclaim as part of your prayer life for the week. Read the
passages of Scripture preceding and following the section you are
to proclaim to better understand the context of the passage.
Meditate on the reading throughout the week, perhaps focusing
on one word or idea which speaks to you. Become so familiar
with the reading that you can tell the story it contains and
communicate that story to the assembly. Read the passage
aloud, paying attention to pronunciation and diction. The
proclamation of Scripture is "spoken song," as the text demands a
certain cadence and tone as well as dynamic control. If the story
has become a part of you, your voice will naturally begin to reflect
the emotional color of the text, and the words you speak will
begin to take on a greater meaning both for you and for those
who hear your voice. It is essential to remember, though, that
liturgy is not a dramatic reenactment of past events. Scripture is

not a script. Liturgy is the active reality of our shared prayer. The proclamation of the Word is a living dialogue that allows us to hear and respond to the God present among us. What we profess as Christians is at once unbelievable, wondrous, and terrifying. If the Word is proclaimed in faith it possesses the power to transform lives.

✚ Practical Considerations

Reading before a mirror with the assistance of a tape recorder can help you to evaluate and improve your proclamation style. Making eye contact with the assembly is an essential part of sharing the Word because all that we do at liturgy is interactive. Reading with the mirror can help to establish a natural way to initiate and maintain that contact. The tape recorder allows you to hear yourself as others hear you and may help you to correct problems with diction, pronunciation, or pacing. Speak slowly and distinctly, project your voice without shouting, and maintain control while you speak. Learn to control your breathing so that your phrasing is dictated by the text rather than by your own need to take a breath. If you have difficulty with this, talk to the music minister in your community. The concepts of breath control in singing apply equally well to speaking. Speak slowly, and when you feel your pace is correct, slow down slightly more to be certain that you will be heard and understood. If possible in your community, it can be helpful to gather with other readers and to videotape each reader while proclaiming the same text. This is an easy way to work out specific problems as well as to encourage and share the positive aspects of this ministry.

✚ Study and Review

Preparing the readings for a liturgy is essential, but before you actually begin your ministry, it is instructive to review the liturgical document *Lectionary for Mass: Introduction.* This document outlines the importance and significance of the Word of God in liturgy. It describes in detail the structure and function of the Liturgy of the Word and provides directives for ministers. Though some may find this text too technical, it is well worth close examination. Along with the other liturgy documents, it forms the foundation of why we do what we do in Catholic worship. *Lector Becomes Proclaimer* by Jerry and Gail DuCharme is an outstanding step-by-step guide to the ministry of the Word. This text guides the reader through the history of proclamation, the act of proclamation, and proclamation techniques. It includes resources for continuing education and formation of readers and provides a framework for growth in this ministry.

Always take time to review the readings before proclaiming them in the assembly, regardless of how familiar a passage is to you. Pay special attention to pronunciation and articulation of any difficult passages. The *Workbook for Lectors and Gospel Readers* (Liturgy Training Publications, published annually) is a helpful resource that contains necessary and insightful information to assist you in this preparation. In addition to the recommendations made earlier with respect to your spiritual preparation, take the time to become intimately familiar with the reading so that you can tell the story with conviction. Do not over-prepare to the point where you become tired of the reading. The story should become new with each telling. A balance may be achieved when the text is both comfortable and stimulating at the same time. When you reach this point, you will easily be able to lift your eyes from the page frequently so that you can connect with the assembly. If you need to use your finger to keep your place, do so. If it is difficult for you to proclaim easily from the lectionary because of the size of the type, the text can be enlarged and inserted into the lectionary; however, never read from the missalette or other such resource. The Word commands a dignity that a missalette cannot provide. Take particular care to check the pronunciation of any unfamiliar words or names, especially those which appear as special intentions. Such sensitivity to family members in the community defines us as an assembly who welcomes those in need. Take your time in preparation; the result will be well worth the time invested.

When you arrive at church before the liturgy, take time to review texts, the general intercessions, and any announcements or changes which may have taken place. Be aware of ritual changes that occur seasonally. For example, the general intercessions usually follow the Creed, but at liturgies at which rites of initiation take place, the Creed may be omitted and the intercessions may take a different form. Being alert to such changes minimizes uncertainty and improves the flow of the liturgy.

✠ Reverence

While you are reviewing the texts of the day, handle the book of Scripture with care. When carrying it or moving it, use both hands. It makes no sense to tuck the lectionary under your arm and stroll through the church chatting with friends before liturgy only to later process in with the book carried with exaggerated reverence. Such behavior causes ritual to appear artificial and contrived. If we believe that this really is the Word of God, it is not difficult to decide how to treat the book containing that Word. What we believe is revealed and reflected explicitly in what we do.

✠ As Liturgy Begins

The entrance procession for a eucharistic liturgy includes a reader who may carry the Book of the Gospels (GIRM 82). The lectionary is intended to remain at the ambo (GIRM 80), although it has become the custom in many communities to process with whichever book will be used at that liturgy. If the Book of the Gospels is carried, the lectionary is not brought in procession to avoid duplication of symbols. As you process through the church, carry the lectionary or the Book of the Gospels with dignity, as high as it is physically possible for you to do. The book should be easily seen by the assembly. Focus your attention on it. We believe that the Lord is present in Word as well as sacrament. Your posture and attitude should be a reflection of the presence that you carry. When you reach the sanctuary, place the lectionary or Book of the Gospels in its place on the ambo or altar and go to your seat. If you do not carry the book in procession, remember to carry whatever worship aid is appropriate to allow you to share in the gathering rites. If you are carrying the lectionary or Book of the Gospels, do not genuflect or bow in reverence to the altar; pause momentarily in reverence and continue. If you are not carrying the lectionary or Book of the Gospels, reverence the altar in an appropriate way, ordinarily with a bow.

✠ Proclamation

Some communities reflect the situation in which several readers proclaim the readings. The ideal would be to have a reader for the first reading, a psalmist for sung proclamation of the responsorial psalm, and a different reader for the second reading.

The deacon would proclaim the Gospel as well as lead the general intercessions following the invitation to prayer by the presider. Such an arrangement reflects more fully the diversity of the assembly and returns the proper role to each minister. However, the reality in some communities is that a single reader reads the texts other than the Gospel and the presider proclaims the Gospel. Regardless of how these ministers of the Word are arranged, the general principles outlined here will apply.

After the opening prayer, go to the ambo for the reading, remembering to reverence the altar (not the presider!) if you pass it. Begin with the citation: "A reading from the book of the prophet Isaiah." It is inappropriate to announce, "Our first reading is...." This is distracting and serves no useful purpose. Conclude the reading with, "The Word of the Lord." Pause (try fifteen seconds—it feels longer than it is!), and return to your seat as the sung proclamation of the psalm begins (the psalm, along with the other texts, should be proclaimed from the ambo). When the psalm is concluded, the next reader should move to the ambo to begin the next reading without delay. Again conclude the reading with, "The Word of the Lord." Do not lift the lectionary as you speak these words. At this point the Word of God has been proclaimed and is alive and present among the people of God. Instead, look up and connect with those who now hold the Word in their hearts. As you sing the Gospel acclamation, return to your place and remain standing and actively listening to the Gospel proclamation. Do not read the Gospel from the missalette while it is being proclaimed because this presents a poor example for the assembly—the Word is meant to be heard and embraced. Reading along distorts this moment.

Be seated as the Word is broken open in the homily. After the Creed, the presider usually introduces the general intercessions. The reader or deacon should begin moving toward the ambo at the conclusion of the Creed. If there is no Creed, the general intercessions begin after the homily, but you should know in advance if this is to be the case. Be careful to read the prayers as they are written and to check in advance the pronunciation of the names included in any special intentions if you are uncertain.

✚ Participation

Participate in all aspects of the liturgy, remembering that you are an example to the assembly. Never act as if your "part" is finished with the conclusion of the Liturgy of the Word. If you refuse to join in prayer, song, or ritual action, the assembly may assume that it is encouraged for them to do the same. "Full, conscious and active participation in liturgical celebrations" (CSL 14) is not merely a dream—it is an ideal that can become reality. Each of us is called to model that ideal, and we should expect and accept no less of the assembly.

✠ Conclusion

As the liturgy concludes, retrieve the book (again using both hands) and move to your place as the procession forms. Process out in the same order as before, and return the lectionary to its storage place for use in the next liturgy. Remember that your role as minister does not end when you reach the door. Stay to continue sharing the Word with your sisters and brothers as they are sent forth to serve the Lord. By your presence, you help to build community and to strengthen the faith that we share. This story makes us one.

✠ Summary

- Prepare yourself with study and practice.

- Spend time with Scripture so that you can tell the story while finding the connections to your own story.

- When you arrive for liturgy, come early and allow yourself some time to prepare and enter into the spirit of the celebration. Take time also to interact with the other ministers and the assembly.

- As the liturgy begins, surrender yourself and the cares of this world as you become one with the community.

- When it comes time for you to read, make contact with those who are listening to you, animate your voice, and let the Spirit work through you. Treat the Word with reverence, recalling that God is always present in the Scripture we proclaim.

- As always, begin and end all that you do with prayer.

✛ Reflection

In the presence of God and of Christ Jesus, who is to judge the living and the dead, and in view of his appearing and his kingdom, I solemnly urge you: proclaim the message, be persistent whether the time is favorable or unfavorable; convince, rebuke, and encourage, with the utmost patience in teaching (2 Tim 4:1-2).

- Is my ministry a proclamation of my own faith, or am I only openly Christian when it is safe or convenient to do so?

- Do I allow the living Word to become a part of my life, or do I simply read and echo the words on the page?

- Am I willing to risk ridicule for the sake of the Word?

- Do I pretend to agree with popular ideas when my heart tells me otherwise?

- Is Christ my judge or do I put the opinions of earthly judges first? Do I insist on what is right and true, or do I remain silent in the face of injustice to myself or others?

May God bless you with every heavenly blessing
and keep you holy and pure in his sight.
May he shower you with the riches of his glory,
instruct you with the word of truth,
form your hearts with the Gospel of salvation,
and enrich you with love for one another,
now and for ever.
Amen (from "The Blessing of a New Lectern," BB 1190).

Ministers of Communion

The cup of blessing that we bless, is it not a sharing in the blood of Christ? The bread that we break, is it not a sharing in the body of Christ? Because there is one bread, we who are many are one body, for we all partake of the one bread (1 Cor 10:16-17).

✚ *Introduction*

As a minister of communion, you have been called to serve the very life of the church, the living Body of Christ. Eucharist is what defines us as community, as a Catholic-Christian people living the command of our Lord, as we make known the promise of the Gospel. The sharing of the Body and Blood of Christ is the source of our collective spiritual life. In your ministry you serve your sisters and brothers by sharing with them the mystery that makes us one.

The following passage is taken from the "Rite of Commissioning Special Ministers of Holy Communion" and expresses the importance and dignity which the church attaches to this ministry:

> You are to be entrusted with administering the eucharist, with taking communion to the sick and with giving it as viaticum to the dying.
>
> In this ministry, you must be examples of Christian living in faith and conduct; you must strive to grow in holiness through this sacrament of unity and love. Remember that, though many, we are one body because we share the one bread and one cup.
>
> As ministers of holy communion be, therefore, especially observant of the Lord's command to love your neighbor. For when he gave his body as food to his disciples, he said to them: "This is my

commandment, that you should love one another as I
have loved you" (adapted from "The Commissioning of
Extraordinary Ministers of Holy Communion," BB 1875).

Remember that your ministry is not something which takes
place for a few moments at Mass or in a home or hospital.
Ministry itself may be a form of prayer, but do not let this become
your only prayer. Prepare yourself daily (or more often) for this
extension and application of your faith. In your prayer, consider
not only yourself, but pray for the community whom you serve. In
this way, you may be better able to recognize the presence of
Christ in one another. This is not to say that lay ministers are to
devote themselves to contemplative prayer to the exclusion of all
other responsibilities and commitments. The beauty of lay
ministry resides in the application of the combined experience of
the secular world and the religious community. Pray often, but
bring this prayer to life through the works that you do so that your
ministry becomes a part of your self.

✚ Preparation

Your preparation for liturgy must extend into your daily life; all
that you do should reflect your commitment. For your ministry to
be real, you will need to nurture a devotion to the Eucharist, a
desire for the real presence of Christ. Your role at liturgy must
never reach the point where you see yourself as "coming to Mass
and giving out communion." Communion is not something which
can be given out; it is a sharing of a most intimate sense. The
Eucharist connects you in a very real sense with the community
of believers. When you speak the words, "Body of Christ" or
"Blood of Christ," you describe not only what you hold in your
hands but also the person you are and the person you see before
you. "The act of Communion, therefore, is also an act of faith. For
when the minister says, 'The Body of Christ' or 'The Blood of
Christ,' the communicant's 'Amen' is a profession in the presence
of the saving Christ, body, soul and divinity, who now gives life to
the believer" (*This Holy and Living Sacrifice* [HLS] 16). Making eye
contact with each communicant and consciously interacting with
each person individually transforms what could become routine
into the reality of ritual. Central to this ministry is the development
of a "sense of the sacred" so that what we do at liturgy never
loses its mystery. If you recall that we are what we celebrate, that

we are called to live each day the death and resurrection, that mystery will become integral and your posture as a minister of the liturgy will reflect this. If this sense of the sacred becomes natural, your presence at liturgy will assume a measured dignity.

✚ *Practical Considerations*

In addition to the essential spiritual preparation, a number of practical preparations are required. In order for your ministry to feel natural in a practical sense, practice handling the vessels with unconsecrated bread and wine until you lose the initial awkwardness that most people feel. Many ministers of communion feel uncomfortable handling the vessels, particularly the cup. Certainly this takes some practice as it is unusual in our secular society to serve another adult person in quite this way. Neither minister nor communicant should fear handling the cup. "[T]he sacred vessels hold a place of honor, especially the chalice and plate, which are used in presenting, consecrating, and receiving the bread and wine. Vessels should be made from materials that are solid and that in the particular region are regarded as noble" (GIRM 289-90). "The vessels should be sturdy, made of materials which are solid and nonabsorbent. Preference is always to be given to materials that do not break easily or become unusable" (HLS 40). This means that the cup should be constructed of a precious material and that it should be substantial in structure. It should be attractive but easy to grasp and handle. It should not be made of a material which is easily broken. One comfortable way to minister communion under this form is to hold the cup primarily with the non-dominant hand (the left hand for right-handed people, and vice-versa), using the other hand to balance the cup. The purificator would be held in the dominant hand. This allows the cup to be extended with both hands and permits the rim of the cup to be wiped and rotated easily. The cup should be wiped and turned after each communicant has received. Practice these motions until they feel natural. This will allow you to be more present to those receiving because your attention will be on them and not on juggling the cup. Whenever you carry or move filled eucharistic vessels, do so with two hands, reflecting the respect you have for the Body and Blood.

In a similar way, handling the plate (or other similar vessel) for the eucharistic bread may require some practice. This vessel should be of a size and shape that is easily held and balanced in one hand. The eucharistic bread is most comfortably held between thumb and the first two fingers, as this allows communion to be given readily in the hand or on the tongue simply by rotating the wrist. Consider what to do if a piece of consecrated bread is dropped before it happens. This is not an occasion for hysteria but rather an event which should be handled with as little fuss as possible. Immediately pick up the consecrated bread and consume it if possible. If it is undesirable to do so for any reason, place the consecrated bread in the hand that is holding the plate and keep it there until you leave to purify the vessel. At that time you may dispose of it according to the custom of your community. The same general process may be applied to a spill of eucharistic wine. Absorb the spill with a purificator (several, if necessary). Rinse the purificator in the sacrarium, then launder the purificator in the usual way. Thinking through the events that may happen at liturgy in advance allows you to adapt to changing situations and will make you more confident in your ministry.

When you arrive for liturgy, take a moment to center yourself and to place yourself in the presence of the Lord. Having done this you may begin the more pragmatic preparation for liturgy in an appropriate frame of mind. Remember to wash your hands before handling the bread and wine. It is a meal that you are preparing. First determine that an adequate amount of unconsecrated bread has been set out for the liturgy. Ideally what we share at liturgy should be consecrated at the same liturgy. Additional communion bread may be consecrated and reserved in the tabernacle if communion is to be taken to the sick. In general, hosts should not be taken from the tabernacle for the purpose of sharing at Mass. Using the same principles, a suitable amount of wine should be measured into the flagon or other vessel. Before using any vessel, check to see that it was properly purified after its previous use. If crumbs or droplets remain, purify the vessel by rinsing with a small amount of water and then consuming that water. Rinse the vessel a second time with a larger quantity of water which may be disposed of in the sacrarium. Once purified, the vessels can be washed with soap and water to maintain their cleanliness and dried before use. Handle these vessels gently as the very nature of their use commands a certain respect. Once you have filled the vessels and set them in place, check that there is at least one purificator for each cup that will be used. Some of these tasks may be performed by the acolyte or sacristan in your community; what is most important is that all is done with care. As you clean and fill and check to see that all is prepared, you may consider taking an emotional inventory so that you can identify and put aside any thoughts or feelings which might distract you or distance you from the community you are to serve. Once all the preparations are made, take a moment to look around the assembly for persons who may be physically challenged or otherwise unable to join in the communion procession. One minister should be assigned to bring communion to these persons in a caring and unobtrusive way. Having completed all of these tasks, join the other ministers. Together greet the people as they enter the worship space. Ready yourself to join in the celebration.

✚ Study and Review

Take some time to learn about the history of the Eucharist as well as the "technical" elements of the Mass, the names of the vessels and linens, their meanings and uses (see the section on servers for recommendations on this). Two excellent resources for this are *The Word and Eucharist Handbook* and *The Sacristy Manual.* Further study might include a review of *This Holy and Living Sacrifice: Directory for the Celebration and Reception of Communion under Both Kinds, Instruction Concerning Worship of the Eucharistic Mystery: Inaestimabile Donum,* and *Instruction on the Worship of the Eucharistic Mystery: Eucharisticum Mysterium.* Although these documents contain a great deal of technical information, continued study will enable your ministry to take on deeper meaning as your understanding of what we do as a Christian people becomes more complete.

✚ Reverence

Treat the consecrated bread and wine with reverence at all times; carry them as the presence of life itself. Although you may come to feel familiar with the elements, a casual attitude is never appropriate. When you pass before the tabernacle, genuflect unless you are carrying the Eucharist itself. Remember always that you are the example, and if your behavior is uncertain or irreverent, you encourage that same behavior among others. Treat the assembly with due reverence as well; your service is to them. Your posture, attitude, and words should reflect the respect that we reserve for the communion that we share. It should be applied equally to both species. "It should never be construed, therefore, that Communion under the form of bread alone or Communion under the form of wine alone is somehow an incomplete act or that Christ is not fully present to the communicant. The Church's unchanging teaching...has witnessed to a constant unity of faith in the presence of Christ in both elements" (HLS 16). When we refer to the Eucharist, whether publicly or privately, the words we use should be chosen with care. Phrases such as "bread stations" are to be avoided, as this speaks of a "fast food" understanding of communion. When ministers of communion decide among themselves who will be responsible for ministering which form, it is never appropriate to say (for example), "I'll give out communion; I don't like the cup." If you are uncomfortable handling either form, practice until that discomfort disappears. When you speak of the elements, use specific, appropriately descriptive terms. When we say "eucharistic bread" rather than "bread," our words reflect our belief in the Christ present in this sacrament. In contrast, if we routinely say "bread and wine" when we mean "Body and Blood," we may begin to diffuse what we believe, and worse, we may unknowingly encourage others to do the same.

✚ As Liturgy Begins

As the liturgy begins, seek in prayer the peace which Christ has promised us. Your participation is the model for the assembly from the very beginning of the liturgy. Your role is not limited to the Liturgy of the Eucharist. In reality, you are always an example both within and outside of liturgy. As you move in procession, join in the gathering song, but do not be so absorbed in the music that you neglect the assembly. You are processing among them, not past or through them. The purpose of this time in the liturgy is to form the assembly into one being, and you can facilitate this by smiling, making eye contact, and expressing the joy of sharing worship. As you approach or pass the altar, reverence it with a bow, but do not exaggerate this posture. It is a simple act of respect, not a time for adoration, and it should not draw attention to you.

✚ *Participation*

When you reach your place in the assembly, continue to sing the gathering song until it is completed. Listen to the proclaimed Word, giving your full attention to the reader. Do not "read along" because this defeats the purpose of proclamation and presents a poor example to the rest of the assembly. When you stand for the proclamation of the Gospel, stand erect, and clearly focus your attention. Do not lean on the pew or seat or in any other way present a casual or distracted attitude. At the conclusion of the Liturgy of the Word, continue to participate fully in the rites of preparation. Your participation in the rite of peace is a time when you may complete your preparation for serving at that particular liturgy. "[B]efore they share in the same bread, the faithful implore peace and unity for the Church and for the whole human family and offer some sign of their love for one another" (GIRM 56b). As you engage in this part of the ritual, make real your desire for reconciliation with God and your community. Express this desire for shared peace in whatever form is appropriate for you and your particular assembly, but never allow it to become an act of habit. Once you have made peace with self, God, and your sisters and brothers in faith, you may approach the altar in service and humility.

✚ *Sharing the Body and Blood*

As you move to the altar as a minister of communion, your motion should be unhurried and with purpose. Questions of positioning or function of various ministers should have been determined before liturgy began, so that at this time each minister can move directly to the appropriate place without any distracting confusion. Your posture of standing is a posture of reverence. Stand without leaning, and focus your attention appropriately. Remember that as you receive communion you form the example for the community. As you take the vessel, reach for it with both hands, carrying it carefully as you move into position. Join in the communion song as you move. As each person approaches you, look directly at the communicant; be sincere and inviting as you interact with each. Don't be afraid to touch as you share communion, as this is a very special form of communication. Don't back away as people approach you, although this may be a natural response. To share in this way, we have to be physically closer to people than usual, and this may cause some natural discomfort at first. Time will eliminate this discomfort if you remember not to move. Take your time; never think that you must rush. If you need a moment to reposition your hands or to wipe the cup or to change the position of the purificator, look down as you do so. The person receiving will likely wait until you look up again before attempting to receive. When sharing the eucharistic bread, remember to check the posture of the person receiving to see whether that person wishes to receive in the hand or on the tongue. Make no judgments about this; never attempt to force someone to receive one way or the other. In the same way, make no judgment about someone who receives under only one form. This decision should be the preference of the communicant.

When finished, carry the vessels to the side table or sacristy, and consume whatever remains. The eucharistic wine is not to be reposed unless it is to be taken to the sick. If a quantity of eucharistic bread too great to be consumed remains, it may be placed in the tabernacle, but this should not be a routine event. In most cases it is preferable to purify the vessels after the liturgy has been concluded to avoid distraction and to allow the ministers some time for prayer.

✠ Conclusion

As the liturgy concludes, join in the song of praise, and carry with you whatever worship aid is needed as the procession forms. Stay to continue sharing the joy we have in communion as you greet and speak with others in your community.

> The life of communion is not a privileged experience available only to Christians, it is realized within the fabric of ordinary human existence. Indeed the events of communion are expressions of our most basic human orientation which draws us out of ourselves and into relationship with others....The mystagogical task of Christian ministry, then, is first to recognize the basic events of communion which are woven into ordinary human existence, and second, to name those events of communion as graced events, as encounters with nothing less than the God of Jesus Christ (Gaillardetz).

✛ Summary

- Prepare yourself emotionally and spiritually to fulfill your ministry.

- Nurture and explore your own spirituality and devotion to the Eucharist. Learn as much as you can.

- When you arrive for liturgy, take time to see that all is prepared for worship.

- Act always with reverence.

- As liturgy begins, allow your entire self to enter into the ritual.

- When you share the Body and Blood, enter into a true communion with those you serve.

- Begin and end all that you do with prayer.

✛ Reflection

May the God of peace himself sanctify you entirely; and may your spirit and soul and body be kept sound and blameless for the coming of our Lord Jesus Christ. The one who calls you is faithful and he will do this. The grace of our Lord Jesus Christ be with you (1 Thes 5:23-24,28).

- Do I truly desire to be "sanctified entirely"?

- What does the concept of holiness mean to me? Is my concept consistent with what God expects of me?

- Am I content to stumble along, trusting that the faith I have will always be enough?

- Do I actively seek to deepen my own faith life or do I assume that this gift of faith is self-sustaining?

- Is my heart open to the presence of God in everyday events?

- Do I close my mind to the Christ present in the faces of those around me, to the mystery of the Spirit, to the wonder of God the creator in the splendor of nature?

- Is my spirit free to live as a Christian?

- Is my life a witness to truth?

- Do I use the gifts I have been granted to further the kingdom on earth?

May Christ, who before the eyes of his disciples
ascended into heaven to prepare a place for us,
and who is present though invisible in the sacrament
    of the altar,
bring you the grace that comes from his sacrifice alone,
to help you and strengthen you always. Amen
(adapted from "The Blessing of a New Tabernacle," BB
1198).

Ministers of Music

O sing to the Lord a new song,
    for he has done marvelous things.
His right hand and his holy arm
    have gotten him victory.
The Lord has made known his victory;
    he has revealed his vindication in the
        sight of the nations.
Sing praises to the Lord with the lyre,
    with the lyre and the sound of melody.
With trumpets and the sound of the horn
    make a joyful noise before the King, the Lord.
Let the sea roar, and all that fills it;
    the world and and those who live in it.
Let the floods clap their hands;
    let the hills sing together for joy
(Ps 98:1-2,5-8).

✠ Introduction

You who are called to the ministry of music are gifted with an enormous challenge as we as church struggle to claim our identity in these times of tension, change, and renewal. Not very long ago, a parish was considered musically complete if it employed an organist to play for some of the Sunday Masses. In contrast, music ministry today requires of you who serve an unprecedented level of commitment, knowledge, and determination to meet the demands of a church in transition. Music is not an accompaniment to liturgy but is a vital part of the life of the church at prayer. With this realization comes the responsibility to serve the people of God in a much broader capacity.

Among the many signs and symbols used by the Church to celebrate its faith, music is of preeminent

> importance. As sacred song united to words it forms a
> necessary or integral part of the solemn liturgy. Yet the
> function of music is ministerial; it must serve and never
> dominate. Music should assist the assembled believers
> to express and share the gift of faith that is within them
> and to nourish and strengthen their interior
> commitment of faith. It should heighten the texts so
> that they speak more fully and more effectively. The
> quality of joy and enthusiasm which music adds to
> community worship cannot be gained in any other
> way. It imparts a sense of unity to the congregation
> and sets the appropriate tone for a particular
> celebration (*Music in Catholic Worship* 23).

The church places great value on the music of liturgy, and you
who serve the liturgy by using your talent to encourage the sung
prayer of the assembly are called to approach this ministry not
only with musical ability and leadership but also with faith and
devotion.

While it may seem nearly impossible at times to coax a
particular community into active participation in the music of
liturgy, on occasion, a single word, verse, or song will reach into
the heart of the assembly. In that instant that group finds itself in
communion with one another—one heart, one mind and one
voice—and it is at this moment that the sung prayer of the people
takes on a life of its own. It is this moment that you as minister of
that prayer are called to nurture and sustain. This is not to imply
that you are the originator of or even the motivation for that
prayer, for it is the Spirit among us who moves us to prayer;
rather, you become the instrument through which the call to
prayer is voiced. To be that instrument, an individual
understanding of the role of the music minister with respect to the
assembly is needed.

> What motivates the pastoral musician? Why does he or
> she give so much time and effort to the service of the
> church at prayer? The only answer can be that the
> church musician is first a disciple and then a minister.
> The musician belongs first of all to the assembly; he or
> she is a worshiper above all. Like any member of the
> assembly, the pastoral musician needs to be a
> believer, needs to experience conversion, needs to

hear the Gospel and so proclaim the praise of God. Thus, the pastoral musician is not merely an employee or volunteer. He or she is a minister, someone who shares faith, serves the community, and expresses the love of God and neighbor through music (*Liturgical Music Today* 64).

✚ Preparation

As a "disciple and minister," your own preparation for liturgy must be complete and should be an ongoing effort. Practice and musical preparation are crucial for these are essential to the discipline of music. Constant attention to your skills as a musician will ensure that the music you share will be of the highest possible quality. You are called to cultivate the talent God has given you and to return that talent to the service of the assembly. The schedule of a full-time music minister is demanding, and time for regular practice and study is difficult to find. For those whose ministry is not full-time, the demands may be different, but the challenge remains the same. Maintenance of your skills is of utmost importance as is the opportunity to meet and interact with others who serve as you do. If you are a director of music ministry, you are responsible not only for yourself but for supporting the growth and development of those who serve with you. In addition to musical ability, you must develop "people skills" so that you can effectively lead others into a deeper understanding and commitment to the ministry of music. If you have a supportive role, you are responsible to the director of music ministry, and that responsibility requires that you prepare your music, that you arrive on time to rehearsals and liturgies, and that you conduct yourself at all times as a minister of the liturgy. Regardless of your role, your preparation must include an active prayer life and a desire to increase your devotion to the cause of supporting the assembly as it becomes one voice in song.

In preparing for liturgy, take time always to focus and center your own thoughts on the task of preparation. As you select and prepare music for liturgy, consider the season, the form and nature of the celebration, and the Scripture that will be proclaimed. Understand the flow and focus of the liturgy so that you can support transitions and climaxes. Music chosen with care should be appropriate and should fit seamlessly into the liturgy. Be sensitive to the repertoire and ability of the community so that the music you choose will be both familiar and comfortable. This is not intended to discourage challenging the community with new music or with music of significant depth. But whatever the music, it should be of high quality (both musically and with respect to the text) and it should be within the ability of the assembly to participate in it. Plan seasonally, and do not fear repetition. Ritual by nature requires repetition, and it takes a great deal of exposure to a piece before an assembly can claim it as its own.

✚ Study

Music ministers are called to be not only musicians but also liturgists and catechists while remaining always sensitive to the needs of the community at worship. "It is highly desirable that organists and other musicians should not only possess the skill to play properly the instruments entrusted to them: they should also enter into and be thoroughly aware of the spirit of the liturgy, so that even when playing *ex temporare,* they will enrich the sacred celebration according to the true nature of each of its parts, and encourage the participation of the faithful" (*Instruction on Music in the Liturgy* 67). At all times, you must be devoted to good liturgy and strive to be a person of prayer. An awareness of the role of music in liturgy throughout the history of the church is essential. Without an understanding of the theology of liturgy, its history, structure, and relevance to our human condition, the music chosen for that liturgy may become arbitrary or even contrary to its intended purpose. A good place to start is to review at least on an annual basis the liturgical documents *Music in Catholic Worship* and the *Instruction on Music in the Liturgy.* These documents describe clearly the church's vision of the role and function of music in worship. They provide a framework for selecting music that will lend cohesion to liturgy. Review of these documents is important not only for directors of music ministry but for other involved musicians—cantors, leaders of song, choir members, and instrumentalists. Presiders and deacons are ministers of music as well, although this is not their primary ministry. These individuals would also do well to explore their own identity with respect to music in liturgy, seeking ways to develop and expand their own level of participation. A useful guide is *The Mystery of Faith: The Ministers of Music.* This text examines the unique role of each minister of music in depth, providing an historical perspective along with excerpts from the liturgical documents that deal with music and liturgy.

Understanding the technical elements of liturgical theology is important, but it is not sufficient because the integration of music into liturgy depends on scriptural relevance. A solid background in Scripture will serve not only to support your own spiritual life but also to form the connections between ritual and sung prayer that give liturgy its unique texture. An understanding of the roots of ritual provides the tools to form the liturgy into a reflection of our identity as a Christian community. At the same time, you must also develop your knowledge of different musical forms and the repertoire of the church. In this way you may embrace in a musical sense the entire history of a dynamic people. It is unjust to ignore the musical ties connecting us to the people of faith who have gone before us, and it is equally unjust to neglect the forms which continue to emerge today. All of our music is valid and reflects who we are in a given time and place. Contemporary music is no less valid than chant; each musical form fills a need, speaks a prayer, and serves a real liturgical purpose. They need not be isolated from one another nor excluded from particular communities. "The musical tradition of the universal Church is a treasure of inestimable value, greater even than that of any other art. The main reason for this preeminence is that, as sacred song closely bound to the text, it forms a necessary or integral part of the solemn liturgy....Therefore sacred music will be the more holy the more closely it is joined to the liturgical rite, whether by adding delight to prayer, fostering oneness of Spirit, or investing the rites with greater solemnity" (CSL 112). If we can come to fear neither tradition nor change, our liturgy will reflect our community identity and will become the prayer that we own. Without deliberate preparation, this ministry becomes performance only, and that vital link to the community at worship is lost. To "sing a new song unto the Lord," we must make our song a new prayer with every voice that joins in until we truly become one body in Christ. By being open in this way, you permit the opportunity for music to be prayer.

✠ *Practical Considerations*

As you seek ways to enable that musical prayer, remember that your role as a minister of music is to encourage and support the song of the assembly. Never deny the people the opportunity to join in singing by replacing congregational parts with solo voices or instruments. Allow the assembly to be heard by carefully ensuring that this sound is not overpowered by instrumentation or amplification. As cantor or leader of song, use your voice, expressions, and gestures to encourage people to sing without attempting to dominate the song. When the choir leads the song, care must be taken to avoid the appearance of performance. At all times the music ministers, instrumentalists, leaders of song, and choir must function as one so that the ministry of the assembly can be supported and uplifted.

Before liturgy begins, review your music to be certain that all is in order (and that all the pages of each piece are there!). All of the music ministers should be in agreement regarding keys, introductions, numbers of verses, signals, tempos, etc. Limit your pre-liturgy practice to the absolute minimum. This stage of preparation should be complete before arriving for liturgy. Check your sound system well in advance of the beginning of the liturgy; sound checks are enormously distracting to those engaged in prayer. Check the positioning of your microphones to be certain that they will not be in the way of instruments or of page turns. Practice page turns, if necessary, until this can be accomplished soundlessly and without causing distraction. As with other liturgical ministers, your attire should be that appropriate to the assembly, being neither distracting nor drawing attention. It is not generally appropriate for ministers of music to be vested, though it is the custom in some communities for choirs, cantors, and leaders of song to wear robes. If so, a simple alb is most appropriate, as the alb is our common baptismal garment. The use of academic-style robes has no root in the Catholic tradition and makes little liturgical sense.

Check with the presider and other ministers for any last-minute changes. Having done all of these, take a deep breath, relax, and allow yourself to enter into the spirit of prayer.

✚ Reverence

The best position for music ministry is in a prominently visible place among the assembly so that you can see and interact with the people. In this position, all you do should reflect the ideal posture for the assembly. As you move through the worship space in preparation for liturgy, do so with an appropriate level of decorum, regardless of how long you have been there or how comfortable you may be in that space. Remember to reverence the altar and the presence in the tabernacle if you pass them. Move deliberately and avoid appearing rushed. When setting up chairs, stands, microphones, etc., do so quickly and quietly if people have begun to assemble. In general, out of consideration for those engaged in prayer, it is best to do all set-up and preparatory work before people begin to assemble for worship. Finally, always reverence the assembly by being welcoming, inviting, and supportive in all that you do.

✚ As Liturgy Begins

When you arrive for liturgy, take a few moments to center your thoughts and to welcome the presence of the Lord. Consciously put aside anything in your mind or heart that might impede your focus at this time. As you begin the gathering song, remember that this is not "traveling music." This is the moment when you directly facilitate the gathering of this assembly into one people. Though you have a unique role, this role should in no way be distant, and your desire should be to become one with the assembly as well. Although the liturgy as it progresses will make constant demands on your attention, try as much as possible to enter into the celebration. In this way your music will truly be prayer, and your prayer will become praise.

✚ Singing the New Song

Your ministry is one of constant service throughout the liturgy as you encourage the assembly to sing the new song which binds us to Christ and to one another. If you are cantor or leader of song, your sense of leadership is as important as your ability to sing. By your posture, your facial expression, and your gesture you communicate your attitude. If your body language is positive, you will engage and support the assembly. The opposite is also true. If you communicate a negative attitude, the assembly will be discouraged. If your music is adequately prepared, you should be easily able to lift your eyes from the page in order to focus on the assembly. Your gesture should be clear and definite as you indicate entrances, but this motion should always be inviting. You are not conducting but encouraging the assembly to embrace and claim the song as their own. Once the assembly has gained confidence you may be able to lead less and blend more, but never betray the trust of the community by abandoning your leadership role when presenting unfamiliar music.

If your role is primarily instrumental, many of these principles apply. If your instrument and ability is such that you can play and sing, doing so will help to support the assembly. If this is difficult for you, focus on your instrument but do not become so absorbed that you fail to notice the presence of the people. If you can take your eyes away from the music to look out among the assembly, the connection you make will greatly enhance your ministry. When you are not playing, join in singing and responding. Your posture as you sit or stand should be prayerful. All that you do should speak of the shared responsibility of all who celebrate to enter actively into the prayer of the liturgy.

✛ Participation

Oddly enough, participation in liturgy may be more of a challenge for those involved in music ministry than for other liturgical ministers. Although you may participate in a complete way in the music of liturgy, your attention is focused on the living celebration, on cues from assembly and presider, as well as on the musical text before you. As a minister of music, your level of participation is crucial. It is absolutely critical that you be involved in all aspects of community prayer. If you limit your interest and attention only to music, you serve the assembly poorly. You also deprive yourself of the emotion and the spiritual energy generated by a people at prayer. If you are focused and aware as liturgy unfolds, you will be better able to support the ritual action with music.

The amount of emotional energy that you expend with each liturgy is great and may become a strain if you minister at many liturgies. Emotional and physical fatigue may combine to limit the amount of attention that you are able to give those parts of the liturgy in which you are not primarily involved. Adequate preparation before liturgy can reduce the difficulty you may experience, but, despite this, you are called to be constantly aware of and responsive to the liturgy as it develops. This does not mean that your participation is less than that of others, but it is different. As with other ministers, you model the posture for the assembly, and so you must give your prayerful attention to all aspects of the liturgy. This is only possible if both your musical and spiritual preparation is sufficient to free you to enter into the spirit of the liturgy. Your own spirituality is always at risk. This is a constant problem for music ministers, for as you focus so intently on fostering and nurturing the prayer of the people, it seems that your own prayer is not supported in the same way. Committing to active participation in the liturgy will help, but it is not the complete solution. Finding a way to balance your own prayer life with the demands of liturgy is necessary, and this solution may be different for each individual, but it is only through this balance that your participation can be real.

The manner of your participation impacts on the entire assembly. Your ministry requires a certain level of discipline so that you are never a distraction. Keeping the area from which you minister neat and free of clutter will help in this regard. Coordinating your own movement with the movement of other ministers and with the assembly reduces distraction. Avoid fumbling with books or pages as much as possible. Turning to face whatever ritual action is taking place will help to direct the attention of the assembly appropriately.

Receiving communion can be awkward without some advance planning and coordination with the ministers of communion. Whenever possible, individual ministers of music should receive at the same time as other liturgical ministers, according to the custom in your community. Choirs and other large groups may need to be communicated separately for logistical reasons, but this should be the exception rather than the rule because all should take part in the communion procession. Whatever the timing, never attempt to receive while singing or playing. It is not usually possible to give your attention to the act of reception while concentrating on supporting and enabling the song of the assembly.

✛ Conclusion

As liturgy concludes, recall that the song of praise that we share as we are sent forth is not an accompaniment to the ritual act of leaving. It need not conclude when the procession reaches the door, but neither should it be artificially prolonged. Whenever possible, liturgical song should be sung in its entirety to preserve the integrity of the text, and this song of praise should not be an exception. When it is completed, stay to talk to the people with whom you have just shared prayer. Their perspective is invaluable, and their response to the music will provide you with a better understanding of the impact the music is having on community and individual worship. Most importantly, this interaction makes ministry real, and the value of that reality must never be underestimated.

✚ Summary

- Understand your role as disciple and minister, and develop that understanding by continuing study and preparation.

- Be familiar with the rites and rituals so that the music will always be a unifying element in the structure of liturgy.

- Base your own formation in Scripture, so that as you support the prayer of the assembly, your own prayer may be supported as well.

- Be complete in your practical preparation, enabling your ministry to be effective while minimizing distractions.

- Be reverent in all that you do, especially regarding the assembly.

- In all things, remember the primacy of prayer, that yours may always be a song of promise and praise.

✚ Reflection

Let the Word of Christ dwell in you richly; teach and admonish one another in all wisdom; and with gratitude in your hearts sing psalms, hymns and spiritual songs to God. And whatever you do, in word or deed, do everything in the name of the Lord Jesus, giving thanks to God the Father through him (Col 3:16-17).

- Is my heart open to the silent music of creation?

- Do I welcome the Lord present in the sung prayer of the people into my life?

- Do I take time to thank God for the gift of my talent and the honor of serving God's people?

- Are my words and actions an inspired reflection of my faith?

- Is the music I share truly a prayer of thanksgiving?

May God bless you,
that your song may be one with
the voices of the redeemed joining in a chorus
    of praise to the holiness of God
as they sing to God in mind and heart.

May the beauty which you create in song and praise
echo always in the hearts of the people you serve, and
may your music lead them always to express prayer
and praise in melodies to the God who is the beginning
and end of all things. Amen (combined and adapted
from the "Order of Blessing of an Organ," BB 1337, and
the "Blessing of Altar Servers, Sacristans, Musicians
and Ushers," BB 1853).

Ministers of Hospitality

If then there is any encouragement in Christ, any
consolation from love, any sharing in the Spirit, any
compassion and sympathy, make my joy complete: be
of the same mind, having the same love, being in full
accord and of one mind. Do nothing from selfish
ambition or conceit, but in humility regard others as
better than yourselves. Let each of you look not to your
own interests, but to the interests of others. Let the
same mind be in you that was in Christ Jesus (Phil
2:1-5).

✠ Introduction

You who are called to be ministers of hospitality are entrusted
with fostering a sense of welcoming and belonging among those
assembled at prayer. You are the first contact made with anyone
who enters the worship space, and you represent the intent of the
community to welcome and embrace all who come to share
prayer. Although functions such as taking up the collection and
seating latecomers are important, your role challenges you
beyond "ushering" to see in every person the face of our Lord.
Yours is a direct service, often a physical one, as you open doors,
smile a greeting, or lend assistance to those in need. You have
the opportunity to be the hands of Christ to the living Body of
Christ. Approach your ministry with diligent preparation, and do
not be discouraged by those who ignore you or refuse your help.
Be watchful for the ways in which you can help to foster the
sense of family among all who worship and especially among
those who are new to your community. Most of all, by your very
presence, be an example of the Christian love which identifies us
and binds us together.

✛ *Preparation*

In preparation for this form of service, it is necessary to develop an understanding of the ministry of the assembly. This ministry of the people is to participate actively in liturgy, praying and praising, sharing and receiving, hearing and responding, and acclaiming in action what we profess in faith. Eugene Walsh said,

> The celebration of Sunday Mass should offer all the people the opportunity of experiencing God, of enjoying the contemplative experience. Everything that is done in planning and celebrating Sunday Mass should move relentlessly and with single-minded purpose toward this goal. Any other goal is not worth the effort....[T]he expression "celebrating community" has a very specific and definite meaning. The term embraces everybody without exception who celebrates a given Mass. It does not mean just the people of the congregation. It means people and priest and all other ministers. This celebrating community as such has a central role and ministry in the work of making Sunday worship come alive and of helping produce the experience of God. No other particular or individual ministry can substitute for the unique ministry of the celebrating community. It is important for us to identify this ministry clearly and to make it become a reality" (*Ministry of the Celebrating Community* 9).

As minister of hospitality, you minister to the entire celebrating community in an active way. By facilitating an atmosphere of welcoming, you enable each person to come to an experience of God. To do this, you must develop a sensitivity to the liturgy as well as a sensitivity to the assembly. If you understand the liturgy, you will be more effective at providing people with the environment they need to worship.

✛ *Study and Review*

If you understand the structure of the liturgy, you will begin to realize when the natural breaks occur which will allow you to seat people or otherwise attend to their needs without disrupting the flow of the prayer. *The Word and Eucharist Handbook* is a valuable guide to exploring and understanding the liturgy. This resource explains with elegant simplicity the origins and significance of each part of the liturgy. A deeper understanding of our common rituals will lead to a greater appreciation of liturgy as a whole. As a minister of hospitality you have a functional role throughout the liturgy, and it is for this reason that your understanding of that liturgy is important. As we gather for worship, you see to it that a welcoming atmosphere is presented. As the liturgy progresses, you ensure that this hospitable environment is maintained. You assist in the rites of preparation by taking a collection or helping with the procession. At communion you may assist those physically challenged to approach the altar or otherwise facilitate the communion procession. As liturgy concludes, your presence assists the assembly as it is sent forth. To perform each of these tasks well, you need to have a solid understanding of the liturgy and a desire to continue to grow in faith.

✚ Practical Considerations

Your understanding and sensitivity should extend beyond the liturgy to each person. Make an effort to meet and interact with people so that you can greet them by name. This does not mean that you should greet those whom you do not know with any less enthusiasm. Among us, there really are no strangers. You are not greeting guests but welcoming members of a family into their home. Know your parish community. Pay attention to what is going on in your parish by reading the bulletin and talking to the staff and coordinators for other ministries. Know the schedule of liturgies so that when people ask questions of you, your response will be direct, helpful, and informative. In being sensitive to the assembly, you should pay attention to the worship environment, the lighting, the temperature, the ventilation, sound system, etc., so that the worship space will remain comfortable. This means that you may need to become familiar with the thermostat controls for heat and air conditioning, light switches, and breaker boxes. Consider what to do in case of emergency; be aware of where the nearest telephone is, where the nearest fire box is, and how to activate emergency lighting if necessary. Know where the restrooms are, which doors squeak, and which windows stick. Some of these tasks may seem almost "too practical" for a liturgical minister, but if your role really is to care for the needs of the assembly, these considerations must not be overlooked.

When seating people, wait until this can be accomplished without interfering with the prayers of those already assembled. For example, at Mass, no one should be seated during Liturgy of the Word. Latecomers should be seated at the end of this part of the liturgy, never during the psalm nor any of the readings. The responsorial psalm is not a break; it is part of the proclamation of the Word. As you become more familiar with the different elements of ritual, you can become more effective at the task of ensuring that all can share fully in the celebration. Your manner and bearing should never be distracting or domineering. When you move through the worship space during a liturgy, do so with quiet dignity. Signaling with two fingers in the air is not an appropriate way to indicate the location of two seats. A better way is to personally and quietly escort two people to their seats. Another example might be during the communion procession, when some communities use ministers of hospitality for "traffic control." Remember that your role is not that of an usher in a theater. Your function is not to herd people but to avoid confusion as people move about. Gently indicate when and where people are to move without blocking the way or otherwise intimidating people. Be conscious of the needs of those who are physically challenged; if they are not able to join the communion procession, you should inconspicuously bring their location to the attention of a minister of communion. If you are responsible for the collection in your community, do so with as little fuss as possible. Your motion should not resemble a parade, and the act of collection is not a procession. Conduct yourself with appropriate decorum and reverence at all times as you move about the worship space.

✛ Reverence

When we speak of reverence, our thinking is sometimes limited to objects. But the people of God are entitled to respect as well, and as a minister of hospitality you are called to reverence the assembly both as a collective group and as individuals. Of course, you will honor in an appropriate way the liturgical objects and elements. But your respect for people must be always evident in your words, your actions, your expressions, and even your thoughts. If you can attempt to see in each person the image of Christ and respond as you would respond to Christ, your service will always be true. Your smile and greeting is a step in this direction, but hospitality does not end there. When you genuinely care about each person and work to provide for all a caring and welcoming environment for worship, you will fulfill your ministry. In this way you reverence and embrace the entire Christian community.

✠ Ministering at Liturgy

When you arrive for liturgy, take time to pray, to center yourself, and to prepare to be a person of welcome. Check the worship space to see that it is free of clutter, that worship aids are neatly arranged, and that the area as a whole appears ready for a celebration. When all is prepared, check with the presider and other ministers for any ritual changes which may require your assistance. Then give your attention to the gathering assembly. As you greet people, do not be afraid to touch or to speak more than a minimal "good morning." Touch is a powerful means of communication, and a handshake or a hug may speak to someone in a way that your words cannot. Your smile reflects your sincerity as you extend the welcome of the community. As the liturgy begins, allow yourself to become immersed in the prayer as it unfolds, even as you continue to be attentive to the needs of all.

✠ Participation

The challenge of this ministry is in remaining attentive to the needs of the assembly while praying and participating among the assembly. It is important for you to be clearly visible, but that does not mean you should be obtrusive. As much as possible, you should be a part of the assembly. Your posture should be neither casual nor overly formal. Avoid leaning on pews, chairs, or walls. If it is the custom in your community to kneel during the eucharistic prayer, it is appropriate for you to kneel or stand, but avoid the "sharpshooter position." This practice of kneeling on one knee while leaning on the edge of a pew for balance is not uncommon, but it is inappropriate. Focus on the ritual action while being aware of the environment around you. Remain in the worship area unless it is absolutely necessary for you to leave. You serve no one by standing outside the doors. Your example of enthusiastic and prayerful participation in the liturgy can be of powerful witness value.

✚ Conclusion

Your preparation for ministry should not be limited to practical considerations but should include an active prayer life. As you develop your understanding of your role in ministering to the community, your service will become a natural extension of your own faith. Your "hospitality" should not begin and end in church. Your Christian example should be evident in all that you do.

✚ Summary

- Develop an understanding of the ministry of the assembly so that you will be better able to serve the needs of the community at prayer.

- Study the form and structure of liturgy so that you may exercise your function in ministry without being a distraction to prayer.

- Be constantly sensitive to people, both as individuals and as assembly.

- Familiarize yourself with the building so that you can help to maintain a comfortable and welcoming worship environment.

- Know your community.

- Treat all people with dignity and respect.

- In all that you do, seek the image and presence of Christ.

✚ Reflection

For this reason I bow my knees before the Father, from whom every family in heaven and on earth takes its name. I pray that, according to the riches of his glory, he may grant that you may be strengthened in your inner being with power through his Spirit, and that Christ may dwell in your hearts through faith, as you are being rooted and grounded in love. I pray that you may have the power to comprehend, with all the saints, what is the breadth and length and height and depth, and to know the love of Christ that surpasses

knowledge, so that you may be filled with all the
fullness of God. Now to him who by the power at work
in us is able to accomplish abundantly far more than all
we can ask or imagine, to him be glory in the church
and in Christ Jesus to all generations, forever and ever.
Amen (Eph 3:14-21).

• Do I truly desire to know Christ?

• Do I search for the presence of Christ in the people I
meet?

• Can I open my heart to accept the fullness of God in
my life?

• Do I know my inner self? Will I permit others to know
the person I really am?

• Am I capable of extending the welcome of Christ to
all people regardless of status?

• Am I willing to serve in humility?

May God bless you, that your presence and care may
offer welcome to all who enter the church, that they
may hear the Word of God, celebrate the sacraments
and heed the voice of Christ: it is Christ who gave
himself to us as the true door to eternal life. Amen
(combined and adapted from the "Order of Blessing of
New Church Doors," BB 1221, and the "Blessing of
Altar Servers, Sacristans, Musicians, and Ushers," BB
1866).

Servers

We declare to you what we have seen and heard so that you also may have fellowship with us; and truly our fellowship is with the Father and with his Son Jesus Christ (1 Jn 1:3).

✚ Introduction

You who are called to serve at the altar share in a ministry that has a long history in the worship of the church. Altar service by the acolyte was at one time part of the "minor orders," considered to be a preparatory stage along the path to the priesthood. The function of the acolyte was to "assist the deacon and to minister to the priest...to attend to the service of the altar, to assist the deacon and the priest in liturgical celebrations, especially in the celebration of Mass...to distribute holy communion, as an extraordinary minister whenever the ministers...are not present, or are themselves unable to distribute holy communion" (CSL 29: Apostolic letter on first tonsure, minor orders and the subdiaconate). The related role of altar server, traditionally limited to boys and men, no longer bears this restriction and so takes on a fuller dimension of Christian service ("Guidelines of BCL," June 1994). The following passage, excerpted from the calling of the candidates to the Institution of Acolytes (*Rites* 2, #4), is an appropriate model of the commitment desired of all who minister at the altar:

> [A]s people chosen for the ministry of acolyte, you will have a special role in the Church's ministry. The summit and source of the Church's life is the eucharist, which builds up the Christian community and makes it grow. It is your responsibility to assist priests and deacons in carrying out their ministry, and as special ministers to give holy communion to the faithful at the liturgy and to the sick. Because you are specially called

to this ministry, you should strive to live more fully by
the Lord's sacrifice and to be molded more perfectly in
its likeness. You should seek to understand the deep
spiritual meaning of what you do, so that you may offer
yourselves daily to God as spiritual sacrifices
acceptable to him through Jesus Christ.

This ministry, visualized in context, is a projection of the
spirituality of the individual interacting in a dynamic way with the
assembly at worship. Although this ministry may be described in
terms of service to the presider, in reality your service is to the
community. Your action enables the liturgy to emerge with grace
and fluidity. As with the other liturgical ministers, your posture and
attitude set the tone and the example for others in the community.
Your purposeful motion speaks of liturgy that was prepared with
care, a celebration in which each person in the assembly
assumes an active role. The cadence of your movement reflects a
prayerful spirit, and as you prepare the altar you image the
humility of a servant.

✠ Preparation and Study

Your preparation for service in this ministry should include
deliberate study of the rites and rituals of the church. Your
familiarity with liturgy will allow you to serve in a more precise
fashion without causing distraction to the presider or assembly.
The best way to begin is to review the texts contained in the
sacramentary. Often overlooked as a reference tool, it describes in
detail the specifics of our shared rituals. The *General Instruction of
the Roman Missal* contained in the sacramentary provides the
framework from which the rubrics may be understood. Many
other texts are available which describe the history and evolution
of the rites of the church, but the sacramentary should be your
primary guide. Take the time to review the ritual any time a
"special liturgy" or an unusual rite will take place. You will deal
more easily with the unexpected events if you have a firm grasp
of the anticipated events. Servers should become accustomed to
the names of the different parts of the church and where the
various items used in liturgy are located. For example, if told to
bring the oil of catechumens to the font, you would likely need to
know that there are three different oils, that they are kept in the
ambry, that the key for the ambry is in the sacristy, and that the

font in question is in the baptismal area of the church. Clearly, it is also essential to know the proper names of the items used in liturgy; otherwise, communication becomes unnecessarily prolonged and these items may not be treated with the appropriate reverence. For example, the term "purificator" has a specific, precise meaning. To call it a napkin or to refer to it as "the thing you wipe the cup with" strips it of its dignity. *The Sacristy Manual* is a treasury of such practical information and includes helpful checklists for common liturgies. Another indispensable source of information about ritual is *The Ceremonial of Bishops*. This text includes descriptions and explanations of many specific aspects of ritual. Although some sections are clearly unique to liturgies at which a bishop presides, the concepts and theory are applicable to many other liturgical situations.

✠ *Practical Considerations*

In order to serve well at individual liturgies, it is important to develop an understanding of the liturgical seasons, their patterns, and the progression that they form. Understanding the general structure of the liturgies of a particular season will make it easier for you to prepare. Paying deliberate attention to the readings of a celebration or season will give you a good feel for the overall focus. Prayerful reflection on those readings will help you to better understand your own role in the liturgy. For example, if the liturgies of the Easter season in your community customarily include a sprinkling rite, you would be certain to check that the water and "sprinkler" are in place before the celebration and know to accompany the presider (if necessary) as he sprinkles the assembly. If you are uncertain about the structure and order of celebration of a particular liturgy at which you are to serve (the Easter Vigil springs immediately to mind!), ask for a walk-through with the presider and other ministers beforehand. Knowing and understanding such things in advance allows your service to be certain, precise, and unhurried.

To serve always with grace should be a continuing goal. To that end, attention to liturgical posture is of great significance. Your movement should not call attention to yourself but should be natural and appropriate to the liturgical event taking place. Take some time in front of a mirror. Practice bowing and genuflecting; check to see that you stand straight, to notice if you wobble when you genuflect, to determine that the presence you project is controlled and reverent. Consider how you walk; is it a well-timed, deliberate movement with purpose, or do you appear to be rushed, confused, or uncertain? When you move, whether it is in procession or across the sanctuary, move half as quickly as what seems natural. What feels painfully slow to you will probably be the right pace to move with dignity and without causing distraction. Practice carrying the processional cross, handling the thurible, and setting the altar before you must do these things publicly. Think about which hand to use for particular actions so that your motion will not be awkward. If you practice these until they become as natural as breathing, your attention can be focused where it is most needed—on the liturgy being celebrated. Once this focus is achieved, you will be able to pray that liturgy as you continue to serve the assembly at worship.

✚ Reverence

As you become more comfortable in your ministry, it is crucial that you resist the somewhat natural inclination to treat what we use at liturgy in a casual way. All that is involved in liturgy—objects, elements, books, and people—assume a sacred identity. For this reason, you must look beyond the ordinary to find the sacred. As you prepare for liturgy, conduct yourself with respect for the reality that these items signify. For example, the sacramentary is more than just a book; it is that book which contains our sacramental texts and which is present at all our sacramental celebrations. It is instrumental in the formation of our community history as it links us with our past and our future. It deserves to be handled with care. By the same argument, the processional cross is more than just a portable symbol. It is the sign and image around which we gather for worship. It should be handled gently when being moved and carried triumphantly when processed. In a similar way, the altar is not just a table but that table on which this Christian assembly offers the eternal sacrifice. Reverence it with a bow and respect it by not using it as a stand for books, glasses, or other trivial items.

The list of such considerations is too lengthy for complete description here, but the underlying principles are consistent. Handle all liturgical items respectfully. Treat the assembly also with respect as you move among them. Consider your appearance to them when you move through the worship space so that your behavior and demeanor will always be appropriate.

This means, for example, that the sanctuary should not be used
as a thoroughfare and that your movement through it should
never be a distraction or disruption to those engaged in prayer
before, during, or after liturgy. In this way you demonstrate and
model your respect for the liturgy and for the people who give that
liturgy life.

✠ As Liturgy Begins

When you arrive for liturgy, take some time to pray, to collect
your thoughts, and to mentally run through the celebration that is
about to take place. If it is the custom in your community, put on
the appropriate vesture, paying attention to the significance of the
baptismal character of the alb you wear. Consult with the presider
and other ministers to coordinate any last-minute modifications to
the ritual. Check to see that the candles are lit (always with a
taper, never with a match!), that the processional cross is in place,
that the credence table has been set with all that is necessary.
Verify the location of the sacramentary and other ritual books so
that you can easily reach them when required. If incense is to be
used, confirm that the thurible is in place, that the boat is filled
with incense, and that the charcoal is lit. When all is prepared,
focus your entire self on the service you offer.

✠ Serving at Liturgy

As you join in the procession, remember that the procession is
a kind of dance with a certain form and meter. This does not
mean that you should "march in time to the music," but your
steps should be deliberate, purposeful, and have a defined
cadence. When you reach the sanctuary, reverence the altar in an
appropriate manner (this will be determined by what you are
carrying as you process). When you pick up the sacramentary or
other ritual book, be certain that the book is right-side up, and, if
possible, open it to the appropriate page. When holding the book,
keep it as steady as possible and at a height that is comfortable
for the presider. When you move with the book, carry it gently,
never tossing it aside when it is not in use. Anticipate and always
be sensitive to the needs of the presider; a glance or gesture
should be all that is required to indicate that action is needed.
Throughout the liturgy, your posture should model that of the
assembly. Avoid distracting movements such as playing with

cinctures or tugging at albs. Coordinate your motion with other movement whenever you can as this will also minimize distraction. Remember that your function is to facilitate uninterrupted prayer. As with other ministers of the liturgy, your attitude is the example and your level of participation speaks volumes.

✢ Participation

Although it may seem that your attention is drawn in many directions, your participation in all aspects of liturgy must be a priority. You should participate with the rest of the assembly whenever it is possible for you to do so. If your hands are occupied by carrying or holding an object (cross, candles, etc.), see to it that whatever worship aid you will need during the liturgy is at your seat. Focus your attention on the primary action that is taking place as your focus is the model for the assembly. This is not always as simple as it might seem because serving well requires that you think one step ahead throughout the ritual. But if your preparation has been complete, you will not be distracted by anxiety or confusion. You will be able to take an active part in the worship of your community, and your ministry of service will be complete.

✢ Conclusion

Above all, serve always in a sense of prayer, remembering that you, too, are part of the assembly. As you serve the assembly, share in the emotion of the people gathered in worship. Spend time with people after liturgy. Sharing insights about our worship experience helps us to grow as ministers and people of prayer. Understanding the perspectives of those whom you serve will help you to function effectively as a ministry of the liturgy.

✢ Summary

- Study and review the rites and rituals until you are comfortable and familiar with the progression and flow of each.

- Base your formation on the seasons of the church calendar and the readings of each season that you may understand the unique character of each season and celebration.

- Learn the terminology of liturgy and develop an understanding of the structure of liturgy so that you can easily assist the presider and other ministers.

- Practice postures, motions, and actions until they become natural.

- Maintain an attitude of reverence with regard to all that is involved with liturgy.

- Serve attentively and participate fully so that liturgy may be a prayerful experience for you and for those whom you serve.

✚ *Reflection*

Therefore rid yourselves of all sordidness and rank growth of wickedness, and welcome with meekness the implanted word that has the power to save your souls. But be doers of the word, and not merely hearers who deceive themselves. For if any are hearers of the word, and not doers, they are like those who look at themselves in a mirror; for they look at themselves and, on going away, immediately forget what they were like. But those who look into the perfect law, the law of liberty, and persevere, being not hearers who forget but doers who act—they will be blessed in their doing (Jas 1:21-25).

- Am I attentive to the Word?

- Do I monitor my own conscience and behavior, or do I turn away from the reflection I see in the mirror?

- Do I seek to incorporate the mystery of the liturgy in my own life?

- Do I truly practice my faith, or is the Creed I profess each week an empty promise?

- Am I willing to take a stand for my faith at home, at work, and among friends as well as among strangers?

May God bless you, that your commitment to serve God and neighbor may deepen. May your role in the liturgy serve as a reminder to all of the servants we are called to be, and may the light of Christ shine always in your heart. Amen (adapted from the "Blessing of Altar Servers, Sacristans, Musicians, and Ushers," BB 1866).

Conclusion

The Holy Spirit dwelling within each of us is a gift so great that without it we are unable even to pray in our own behalf. Empowered by this indwelling Spirit, our faith takes life and assumes an unlimited potential for growth. But without sustenance, this seed of faith that we have will not thrive. By opening our hearts and minds to the goodness around us we are better able to embrace the Christ who calls us to live in freedom and truth. By giving back what we have been given we say "Amen" to all that Christ has taught and promised. In service that is given in love without a desire for recognition, we witness to the truth of the Gospel. In this way we share in all that is holy as we wait for the perfection of God's kingdom.

Death holds no power over a follower of Christ. In Christ there is only life, and so we willingly entrust our lives to his care. But if we accept this promise of everlasting life, we are called to accept the name of Christian, to reject what is evil in this world and profess publicly our belief in the resurrection of our Lord. In the rituals of initiation these words are heard repeatedly. For those of us baptized as infants, these words are spoken by our parents and godparents, later to be repeated by our own tongues when our initiation is completed. Each time we renew these baptismal promises, these same words are repeated as they become a part of our very being. We may take great strength and courage from the triumphant sound of the Creed being professed in the assembly of believers. But the real test of our courage and faith comes when we profess these words in action, in the world, among believers and non-believers alike.

Final Reflection

The ministries of the Church are in our hands. We are called to be a servant community: a community that recognizes the natural leaders that God has given us, a community that dialogues with those leaders, a community that invites those leaders and all to sit together at the table of the Lord. May our vision be to receive one another as Christ received the holy woman of the gospel. May we work together to realize the dream of being united around one table, receiving together the bread that gives us life. Let us see one another in communion (Matovina 359-360).

For by the grace given to me I say to everyone among you not to think of yourself more highly than you ought to think, but to think with sober judgment, each according to the measure of faith that God has assigned. For as in one body we have many members, and not all the members have the same function, so we, who are many, are one body in Christ, and individually we are members of one another. We have gifts that differ according to the grace that was given each of us: prophecy, in proportion to faith; ministry, in ministering; the teacher, in teaching; the exhorter, in exhortation; the giver, in generosity; the leader, in diligence; the compassionate, in cheerfulness. Do not lag in zeal, be ardent in spirit, serve the Lord. Rejoice in hope, be patient in suffering, persevere in prayer. Contribute to the needs of the saints; extend hospitality to strangers (Rom 12:3-8,11-13).

- Am I aware of the gifts God has given me?

- Am I willing to offer these gifts in the service of God's people?

Final Reflection

- Do I offer these things eagerly or reluctantly?

- Do I become angry at the difficulties I encounter in my ministry?

- Do I pray regularly and spontaneously?

- Do I share what I have with those in need?

- Do I accept the hospitality of others when I myself am in need?

- Will I allow myself to be ministered to or do I reject those who reach out to me?

May the God of glory
bless you who respond to the needs of your faith
  communities
as you commit yourselves to service in liturgical
  ministry.
May your ministry be fruitful
and the worship you share be pleasing
  in the sight of God. Amen
(adapted from the "Blessing of Altar Servers, Sacristans, Musicians, and Ushers," BB 1868).

This is my commandment, that you love one another as I have loved you. No one has greater love than this, to lay down one's life for one's friends. You are my friends if you do what I command you. I do not call you servants any longer, because the servant does not know what the master is doing; but I have called you friends, because I have made known to you everything I have heard from my Father. You did not choose me, but I chose you. And I appointed you to go and bear fruit, fruit that will last, so that the Father will give you whatever you ask him in my name. I am giving you these commands so that you may love one another (Jn 15:12-17).

References and Suggested Reading

Book of Blessings. Collegeville, Minnesota: Liturgical Press, 1987.

Catholic Household Blessings and Prayers. Washington, DC: United States Catholic Conference, 1989.

DuCharme, Jerry, and Gail DuCharme. *Lector Becomes Proclaimer.* San Jose: Resource Publications, 1985.

Fleming, Austin. *Preparing for Liturgy: A Theology and Spirituality.* Washington, DC: The Pastoral Press, 1985.

Gaillardetz, Richard R. "In Service of Communion: A Trinitarian Foundation for Christian Ministry." *Worship* 67, no. 5 (September 1993): 428.

General Instruction of the Liturgy of the Hours. New York: Catholic Book Publishing Co, 1975.

Guardini, Romano. *"How Firm a Foundation: Voices of the Early Liturgical Movement.* Kathleen Hughes, RSCJ, ed. Chicago: Liturgy Training Publications, 1990.

Instruction on the Worship of the Eucharistic Mystery: Eucharisticum Mysterium. English ed. Boston: Daughters of St. Paul, 1980.

Instruction Concerning Worship of the Eucharistic Mystery: Inaestimabile Donum. English ed. Boston: Daughters of St. Paul, 1980.

Johnson, Lawrence J. *The Mystery of Faith: The Ministers of Music.* Washington, DC: National Association of Pastoral Musicians, 1983.

———. *The Word and Eucharist Handbook.* Revised ed. San Jose: Resource Publications, 1993.

Liturgy Documents: A Parish Resource. 3rd ed. Chicago: Liturgy Training Publications, 1991.

Liturgy of the Hours. New York: Catholic Book Publishing Co, 1975.

Matovina, Timothy M. "Ministries and the Servant Community." *Worship* 67, no. 4 (July 1993): 351-360.

Rademacher, William J. *Lay Ministry: A Theological, Spiritual, and Pastoral Handbook.* New York: Crossroad Publishing Co., 1991.

Rite of Christian Initiation of Adults. Study Edition. Collegeville, Minnesota: Liturgical Press, 1988.

References and Suggested Reading

Rosser, Aelred. *Workbook for Lectors and Gospel Readers*. Chicago: Liturgy Training Publications, 1992.

Ryan, G. Thomas. *The Sacristy Manual*. Chicago: Liturgy Training Publications, 1993.

Sourcebook for Sundays and Seasons. Chicago: Liturgy Training Publications, 1992.

Walsh, Eugene, SS. *The Ministry of the Celebrating Community*. Daytona Beach, Florida: Pastoral Arts Associate of North America, 1986.

———. *A Theology of Celebration*. Daytona Beach, Florida: Pastoral Arts Associate of North America, 1986.

More Liturgy Resources

THE USHER'S BOOK OF THE MASS

Editors of MODERN LITURGY

Paper, 80 pages, 4" x 7", ISBN 0-89390-364-7 *Bulk Prices Available*

Help your ushers understand the basics of the Mass — and why their role is so important. This book will tell ushers about the structure of the Mass, the symbols used in the Mass, and the way in which their ministry contributes to the flow and prayerfulness of the Mass. Easy and fun to read, the book fits easily in a jacket pocket or purse.

LECTOR BECOMES PROCLAIMER

Jerry DuCharme & Gail DuCharme

Workbook Edition: Paper, 80 Pages, 8½" x 11", ISBN 0-89390-158-X
Original Edition: Paper, 74 pages, 4" x 6", ISBN 0-89390-059-1 *Bulk Prices Available*

Help lectors understand the difference between proclaiming and reading the Scripture lections with these helpful preparation techniques and delivery tips. Workshop edition shows you how to implement a series of training workshops.

THE YOUNG SERVER'S BOOK OF THE MASS

Kenneth Guentert

Paper, 80 pages, 4" x 6", ISBN 0-89390-078-8 *Bulk Prices Available*

Here is the history of the Mass in the language of young people. With this background, servers can understand why they do what they do. You'll be pleased with the results: they'll feel and act like a special part of the liturgy.

MODERN LITURGY ANSWERS THE 101 MOST-ASKED QUESTIONS ABOUT LITURGY

Nick Wagner

Paper, 144 pages, 5½" x 8½", ISBN 0-89390-369-8

Everyone has a question about liturgy — from the basic (What's a missal?) to the practical (Where should the presider preach from?). Now you can provide answers to those questions and more from the editor of *Modern Liturgy* magazine. Includes historical and theological background of current liturgical practices in a friendly format and style.

Call 1-800-736-7600 for current prices.
See last page for ordering information.

Ministry Programs

MINISTRY TO THE HOMEBOUND: A 10-Session Training Course
Kent C. Miller

Paper, 176 pages, 8½" x 11", ISBN 0-89390-268-3

This resource provides educational material along with a guided group process to help communion ministers, deacons, persons charged with visiting the sick, and pastors organize an effective program of regular and meaningful visitation to persons who are ill and homebound. Here is everything you need for a ten-session course on ministering to the homebound: background on building a caring ministry, session plans, and handouts you are allowed to photocopy.

GRIEF MINISTRY: Helping Others Mourn
Donna Reilly Williams & JoAnn Sturzl

Paper, 200 pages, 5½" x 8½", ISBN 0-89390-233-0

GRIEF MINISTRY FACILITATOR'S GUIDE
JoAnn Sturzl & Donna Reilly Williams

Paper, 144 perforated pages, 8½" x 11", ISBN 0-89390-227-6

Grief Ministry: Helping Others Mourn fills the need for an up-to-date resource that combines spiritual and psychological insights about grief-work. It covers general aspects of grieving, empathy, communication, listening, and prayer. The authors share insights on handling difficult situations, including such special cases as suicide, the death of a baby, job loss, AIDS, and divorce.

The *Facilitator's Guide* shows how to set up a program to train grief ministers using *Grief Ministry: Helping Others Mourn* as a textbook. The guide includes group listening and role-playing exercises, scenarios for discussion, a resource listing, and useful handouts with photocopy permission included.

Order from your local bookseller, or contact:

Resource Publications, Inc.
160 E. Virginia Street #290 - LE
San Jose, CA 95112-5876
800-736-7600 (voice)
408-287-8748 (fax)